GRIEF IN SCHOOL COMMUNITIES

Effective support strategies

Louise Rowling

Open University Press
Buckingham · Philadelphia

Open University Press
Celtic Court
22 Ballmoor
Buckingham
MK18 1XW

email: enquiries@openup.co.uk
world wide web: www.openup.co.uk

and
325 Chestnut Street
Philadelphia, PA 19106, USA

First Published 2003

A catalogue record of this book is available from the British Library

ISBN   0 335 21115 1 (pb)   0 335 21116 X (hb)

Library of Congress Cataloging-in-Publication Data
    Rowling, Louise.
        Grief in school communities: effective support strategies / Louise Rowling.
            p. cm.
        Includes bibliographical references and index.
        ISBN 0-335-21116-X (hbk) – ISBN 0-335-21115-1 (pbk.)
    1. Grief in children.   2. Grief in adolescence.   3. Loss (Psychology)
in children.   4. Loss (Psychology) in adolescence.   5. Grief in children
–Study and teaching (Elementary)   6. Grief in adolescence–Study and
teaching (Secondary)   7. Loss (Psychology) in children–Study and teaching
(Elementary)   8. Loss (Psychology) in adolescence–Study
and teaching (Secondary) I. Title.
BF723.G75 R69 2003
155.9'37–dc21   2002074905

Typeset by Graphicraft Limited, Hong Kong
Printed in Great Britain by Biddles Limited, Guildford and King's Lynn

Contents

Foreword

Foreword

Until recently the impact of bereavement on young people was considered only in terms of its effect upon the adult they might become rather than concern for the experiences and needs of the young people themselves (Doka 1989). The last decade has seen increasing professional and public interest in the needs and rights of bereaved young people and their families. However, this increasing awareness has not been matched by the coherent development of appropriate support structures (Stokes *et al.* 1999). Specialist bereavement services are being established piecemeal in the absence of national policy or planning and with no agreed standards or monitoring. Young people's chances of finding what they need are hit and miss; provision is patchy and quality variable.

All young people have a powerful drive to ask questions and to try to make sense of the world in which they live. All young people will experience loss: the death of a pet, moving house, failing an important exam, watching news of disasters on television, ending a love relationship, experiencing the separation or divorce of parents. Adults would prefer that young people did not. Adults may be struggling with their own grief. They may find it hard to know how to respond to their children's needs for information and emotional support, or distressing to witness their efforts to unravel issues of justice and meaning. As one mother whose husband had a terminal illness said of her young daughter's reactions: 'It hurts to watch my child in pain. But then I realised that it isn't a choice of whether she will hurt or not, but whether I will know about it.' (Christ 2000). I remember my own sense of inadequacy in the face of the questions of a 6-year-old boy whose mother had recently died of cancer and whose pet cat now had cancer and was suffering with intractable symptoms. He said to me: 'Black cat is dying. They're going to kill black cat. If they put animals to sleep why don't they put people to sleep?' In their efforts to protect young people, and of course themselves, adults often leave them confused and alone, unprotected from their fears and fantasies.

Grief is not an illness. It is a normal and inevitable part of human existence. All young people will have to find ways to incorporate the experience and its meanings into their lives. In doing so many will discover new personal resources and maturity. Helping young people to confront and learn about loss, grief and death, and to develop emotional capacity and intelligence, is too important to leave until moments of personal or community crisis. Their loss experiences do not occur in a separate and parallel universe, although adults sometimes behave as if they do. An integrated and comprehensive approach is vital if we are to ensure that all have access to support at the level they want and need, when they need it. We must find the right balance between the expert, professional therapeutic intervention necessary for a few individual young people and their families and a societal agenda that promotes general loss education in the school curriculum and that trains, resources and supports the professionals who already meet grieving children in their everyday lives such as the police, family doctors, health visitors and teachers.

An exclusive focus on the separate development of sophisticated mechanisms to try to target those young people at risk and to single out those labelled as vulnerable for individual help delivered by experts from outside specialist agencies, can both disempower and stigmatize. Social context is vital; it is through the social environment and social interaction that young people begin to make sense of their loss experiences. Research demonstrates that social support helps people to manage life crises and that young people need help from peers and adults in their community as well as their parents (Worden 1996). Experts can only ever be present for brief snapshots of time in a young person's life. We know that young people revisit and reinterpret loss experiences over time (Klass *et al.* 1996). They need ongoing support from their families, communities and friends as they do so. To provide this the whole social environment will itself need structures, information, education and support.

In over 25 years of working with young people experiencing loss it has been emphasized to me over and over again that the school community has a central role in the task of supporting young people and their families. School is, after all, the primary focus of social interaction for young people and the context in which most of their formal learning occurs. Louise Rowling's book offers a powerful manifesto about why and how schools can also become safe places to begin the protective process of social and personal learning. She describes a health promoting school framework, placing the school at the heart of a carefully planned network of support. She emphasizes not just death, but the wider context of loss that will allow all young people to engage actively with the issues. Were her model to be adopted it could help to prevent difficulties escalating and provide a filter for referral for more specialist support where necessary.

The whole style and tone of Louise Rowling's book mirrors its message. Inclusive, wide-ranging, sensitive and practical; it has suggestions about curriculum development, critical incident management and creating effective pastoral communities, as well as helping upset children in the classroom, running support groups and meeting parents. The arguments are solidly grounded in a clear discussion of theoretical concepts and a careful synthesis of relevant research. Most persuasive in the case she presents is her own research. In common with all the best work it is based on her detailed and respectful listening to and distillation of the powerful, personal and day-to-day experiences of teachers, young people and their parents. The voices speak for themselves. The lessons for us are clear. From my United Kingdom base they sound like a wake-up call. A number of recent and well-publicized school-based tragedies provide a stark reminder that preparation and planning are vital. However, good pastoral care structures and effective links with outside community agencies are not just plans to be put in place when disaster strikes. They matter all the time and must be developed, modified and sustained over time otherwise young people's personal loss experiences and grief may remain hidden and unsupported.

Louise Rowling offers a model of community teamwork, of the 'joined up thinking' currently so in vogue with politicians, with schools and teachers taking a leadership and facilitation role. Crucially, she also demonstrates a real understanding of the personal and professional pressures on individual teachers and the responsibilities and demands placed upon headteachers who are often lonely and unsupported leaders and managers. She emphasizes that if the model is to work, schools and teachers need funding and a system of care. She underlines the need for boundaries and structures for safe containment at all levels and that more specialized roles should only be taken on by those who feel comfortable with them. In short she reminds us about the importance of care for the carers.

Young people need acknowledgement and deserve respect. They have a right to be listened to and to be supported. They should not have to go  it alone. Young people have an enormous capacity to grow in response to the challenges of loss. They are resilient, but as Louise Rowling says this does not mean that 'they are not affected, but that they can bounce back with support'. We cannot make a world in which young people will not experience loss, we can offer them support as they do so. Helping them to express and manage feelings of loneliness, insecurity, anger and sadness can provide profoundly important lessons that they take with them as they move through life and experience further losses in the future. Louise Rowling has offered a possible map for the provision of support. The precise route taken must depend upon individual communities, their cultures and resources. However the challenge is there for us all.

Barbara Monroe
Chief Executive of St Christopher's Hospice
London, UK and Director of 'Candle' – a bereavement
project for young people and their families

Preface

This book is an essential guide for all members of a school community and the people who may need to be informed about how to be supportive in times of crisis. It aims in one volume to create a reference for school community members for managing grief in primary and secondary schools. It represents over 20 years of research, teaching, reading, discussion and reflection by the author in several countries. The book describes shifts in practice that are occurring in different parts of the world. School students have been the focus of research and interventions in the field of loss and grief: a student is dying, a student dies, a child is coping with the death of a loved one and, more recently, the impact of a critical incident in which one or more students die. These events are undoubtedly powerful instigators for theorizing, research and practice. But a shift has occurred based, in the last decade or two, on the need to see these loss experiences as being interpreted through social interaction and the social environment of the school and on a range of losses not just death. Another shift has occurred in Australia, locating grief in the wider health field and altering the focus from the pathology of grief to the normality of grief. This shift involves placing loss and grief, as a normal life experience, within the mental health promotion field. This has broadened the scope for supportive action.

The book is based on extensive research using surveys, interviews, participant observation, comments from evaluations of workshops and analysis of documents. From this, the concept of the disenfranchised grief of teachers was articulated for the first time. A conceptual descriptive approach is adopted to link the research literature with frameworks and the data. These frameworks and their rationale are presented at the beginning of each chapter. They can be used to inform and shape school responses, given each school's particular history, culture and circumstances. The narratives of school community members, teachers, administrative staff, students, parents, headteachers and community resource people are used verbatim to illustrate beliefs, experiences and the meaning created from the events encountered. Their words are presented in italics throughout the book. These personal accounts are the real lives of the participants as they experienced events and as they reflected upon them. That is, they are concerned with the day-to-day functioning of schools where loss and grief occurs, not the study of abnormal situations and problems. The book relies on readers drawing 'naturalistic generalizations', by recognizing a link between other people's experience and their own.

The first two chapters document the organizing theoretical and conceptual frameworks and include a concise account of young people's reactions to loss. Teachers as important members of the school community are the focus of Chapter 3; their duty of care and connections with young people shape their supportive actions. Chapter 4 focuses on the classroom, highlighting issues surrounding the teaching of loss and grief. Chapter 5 looks at critical incident management, which may be the entry point to this book for many school personnel. Comprehensive discussion is given of the issues that arise in these emotionally charged events. An underpinning theme of the book, the need to create a supportive school environment for grief, is the focus of Chapter 6. This could be the starting point for a programme aimed at creating a school climate that accepts grief and supports grieving individuals and groups. Chapter 7 presents, for the first time, the accounts of headteachers in Australia, England and Canada of being a leader and a manager when their school experienced a critical incident. It is essential reading for all headteachers and their deputies. Chapters 8 and 9 extend the discussion to families and partner agencies. A theme in these chapters is the need for collaborative action. Chapter 10 briefly describes special cases, suicide, chronically ill young people, indigenous and migrant children and the particular circumstances of grief in special schools, where young people often with a limited lifespan are educated and supported. Chapter 11 looks at disenfranchised grief in schools, elucidating how the environment of schools can be the basis of this phenomenon. The final chapter describes the training that is required to achieve the environments and supportive actions proposed in the earlier chapters.

Each chapter concludes with summary points and practical suggestions. Titles for further reading are provided that provide more in-depth accounts of some of the issues raised. The book is written for several audiences. Some chapters may be read singly or in any combination. However, the chapters are in a sequence to provide a logical development. Cross-referencing is used to indicate where issues are covered in more detail elsewhere in the book. In most cases throughout the book, 'young people' is used as a generic term for both children and adolescents. A glossary is included, as the book is not only aimed at a multidisciplinary audience but also at people in different countries, where different terms are used in school settings. The word 'coping' is avoided in the text because of its negative connotations associated with 'just managing'. People grieve actively and they use many strategies to adapt to their loss.

Although schools will inevitably face traumatic events and school personnel will encounter loss in their lives, it is my hope that, through this book, individuals and school communities will be able to create environments in which grief, while a difficult experience, is seen as a normal life event.

Louise Rowling
University of Sydney

Acknowledgements

This book would not have been possible without the help of a number of people. I thank Susette and Vicki for their ongoing support and in the many ways in which they assisted me; and to my colleagues and friends, all of whom helped me over many years. My two cats Bilbo and Babe, provided diversion when I needed a break from writing and kept life in perspective for me, when I was in danger of becoming too absorbed in my work.

To the participants in my research, thank you for the trust you placed in me, willingly telling me your often painful stories. I hope the insights documented in this book honour the support and trust I have received.

Copyright permission:

'Dunblane' by Andrew MacFarlane. Reprinted with the permission of the New South Wales Teachers' Federation, Publications Division.

Sections of Professional Development in Chapter 12. Originally published in Rowling, L. (2000) *MindMatters: A Whole School Approach to Loss and Grief.* Canberra: Mental Health Promotion Branch, Commonwealth Department of Health and Aged Care (available at http://www.curriculum.edu.au/mindmatters) Reproduced with permission of the Mental Health Branch, Commonwealth Department of Health and Aged Care.

Disclaimer:

This book provides a review of research and examples of practice identified through research and consultation by the author and other professionals. The publisher and the author cannot be held responsible for any error or omission in the information nor outcome of use of the information.

CHAPTER 1

Frameworks for a comprehensive approach to loss and grief in schools

Introduction

The immediacy and real-life coverage as well as the graphic recreation of events in New York City on 11 September 2001 has shifted **young people's** personal and vicarious experience of death and **grief**. New forms of 'protection' are needed, not just through family support but also within school communities.

The image of death created by the media is a distorted view that is violent and tragic, heightening the fear of it. Young people are being educated about grief, but the context of this education is trauma and tragedy, not the 'normality of grief'. The value of a 'normality' approach to grief is that it can lessen feelings of insecurity, loneliness and self-consciousness when young people experience **loss**. Schools have a role to play in challenging the negative view portrayed in the media, that loss never has positive outcomes. A comprehensive approach to loss and grief can develop important life skills in young people and can strengthen school communities.

In the past, the focus of much work on grief in schools has been negative, with grief being seen as a problem that has to be 'cured'. Part of this 'problem' orientation comes from the timing of the entry point for the consideration of loss and grief, usually during crisis management in schools experiencing **critical incidents**. From a mental health perspective, grief has been part of an individual 'illness' orientation, emphasizing 'counselling'. There has been a steady encroachment of professionals (Barnard *et al.* 1999). This construction of grief in a 'disease' framework distorts grief support, focusing on causative factors, vulnerable groups and interventions aimed at improving individual functioning, often undermining individual and school community restorative processes. A more positive approach to loss and grief is to consider protective factors, whole communities and prevention in terms of individual and collective resilience, learned resourcefulness and social determinants of grief support. In this view, schools are safe places to confront, learn about and manage grief. This arises from the recently articulated concept of mental health promotion for young people that involves a more positive orientation (Rowling *et al.* 2002). A key shaping element in the development of mental health promotion has been Antonovsky's (1987) concept of 'salutogenesis' – the study of health rather than pathogenesis, the study of illness.

Parallel shifts in focus have occurred in the field of grief, with greater knowledge of the sociological factors that influence the outcome of loss. In relation to schools, the re-focus is on the school as a social institution for personal and social learning, as well as academic outcomes, for students. The experience of loss as a justification for its inclusion in the curriculum has been echoed by many (LaGrande 1988; Weekes and Johnson 1992). The purpose of such a curriculum is broad – 'enhancing human development and quality of life' (Weekes and Johnson 1992: 220). This approach views schools as 'settings' that can enhance mental health.

Past approaches to loss and grief in schools

Globally, school communities are currently experiencing traumatic events that have the potential to affect the mental health of those involved, the academic progress of students, the worklife of teachers and the public perception of schools as safe, physical and psychosocial environments. Such events result in students experiencing death and trauma to a greater extent than in the past, when their exposure to loss and grief was more likely to be through the death of family members. Schools have traditionally 'cared' for the psychosocial needs of students. As a result of changing experiences and increasing knowledge of the impact of grief on children, various waves of activity have addressed loss in schools.

A first wave focused on children's experience of death, ensuring a grieving student had access to outside counselling, with perhaps a teacher supporting the young person day to day and sometimes teaching about death in the curriculum. There are several reasons why this has proved unsatisfactory. The emotionality of these issues has meant that the teachers involved would have benefited from training and the opportunity for a sharing of feelings and experiences of the teaching with colleagues. Additionally, effective support for a student requires awareness and a response from staff in combination with parents. Also, links may not have been established with health professionals providing counselling, so it is probable that there was no continuity of care. A sole focus on a student's experience of death misses their other loss experiences and ignores all the other members of the school community who might be impacted by death.

A second wave of activity broadened the approach to grief. Teachers introduced stories with grief themes and discussions about animal life cycles for younger students, and lessons about coping with changing relationships for adolescents, usually after a loss had been experienced. Support groups conducted by outside agencies were used as referral points for young people encountering problems coping with grief. **Pastoral care** was provided for individual students. In the case of traumatic incidents, sole reliance was placed on outside specialists or a trauma team (Leenaars and Wenckstern 1998). This often resulted in the school community feeling disempowered. It also failed to recognize the school community as a social institution with its own history, culture and day-to-day practices. This second wave provided death and grief education within the curriculum, support for those experiencing a loss and treatment for those at risk of experiencing longer-term problems. These aspects of care are usually labelled 'prevention', 'intervention' and 'postvention' (Petersen and Straub 1992). They represent a fairly typical framework for past public health interventions, already documented as being applicable for suicide (Centers for Disease Control 1988; Berman and Jobes 1997), traumatic events (Nader and Pynoos 1993) and grief (Klicker 2000).

The current wave of activity has built upon a number of developments. These include:

- delineation of the 'social construction of grief' (Averill and Nunley 1988);
- prevention and postvention strategies that are associated with good outcomes after disasters (Centers for Disease Control 1992);
- the emotional reactions of young people involved in critical incidents (Nader 1996);
- research evidence that young people need an unbiased friend and significant others to talk with (LaGrande 1988);
- the preventive mental health potential of planning to cope with life crises (Parkes 1988);
- research evidence of the role of social support in helping grieving people (Marris 1975; Vachon and Stylianos 1988; Cutrona *et al.* 1990; Nader 1996);
- the potential role of the school community as a supportive network (Petersen and Straub 1992; Yule and Gold 1993; Stevenson 1996; Leenaars and Wenckstern 1998);

- the need to understand how people's assumptive worlds are challenged by loss experiences (Janoff-Bulman 1989); and
- the importance of the 'meaning' of loss events to individuals and communities (Stroebe *et al.* 1993).

A new direction is required that focuses on the social context of school communities that grief and critical incidents are embedded in. A proactive rather than a reactive approach to coping with grief is also needed. The value of this proactive approach was highlighted by Dyregrov (1991: 80): 'Experience has shown that mental preparation and planning before a death or other critical event occurs, leads to a much better handling than if one "takes things as they come"'.

This new approach recognizes that grief and loss in school communities have special meanings to those communities – the loss is constructed within them and needs to be managed within that context, although outside resources may be utilized. The social context of grief is the starting point for designing interventions. In this environment, clinicians act as advocates for the school and provide links with outside services for those who are experiencing grief and trauma. The focus of activity shifts to the adoption of a comprehensive management strategy that involves people – their practices, philosophy, knowledge and comfort about grief – and school community structures, programmes and policies.

A wider context for loss and grief encourages the development of a comprehensive approach to grief that accepts the normality of grief in a school community. Normal in this context means natural, not a prescribed pattern of behaviour. To develop a comprehensive approach, frameworks are needed for planning ways to address these issues. It is possible that by providing such a structure, school personnel will be less anxious and be more proactive. Research indicates that this approach, while in its infancy in England, is better developed in Australia (Rowling and Holland 2000).

In this chapter, several theoretical orientations and frameworks synthesized from research and practice provide guidance for planning at system and school levels. These include a new public health approach, the health promoting school, school-based mental health promotion, the personal and social aims of schools, and sensitive issues in schools. These frameworks and theoretical orientations are used to underpin subsequent chapters in this book, with interweaving themes emphasizing the interaction of theory and practice.

Loss and grief in a public health framework

An ecological perspective is adopted in the 'new' public health (O'Connor-Fleming and Parker 2001). This involves recognition of people's health being determined by their environment, not merely by identifying risk factors (being bereaved) that can be targeted and cured. For school communities, this shifts the emphasis from a focus on providing counselling services to individuals and groups, to a focus on how the school as a social institution should create conditions conducive to positive mental health outcomes. In this approach, the school as an organization is the starting point and the role of public policy (and by necessity school developed policies) is crucial. These can provide a normalizing and affirming environment for grieving young people (Johnson 1989) and a legally accountable and ethically responsible educational context for responding to critical incidents (Deaton and Berkan 1995). Loss and grief research and interventions are infrequently linked to mainstream preventive health approaches. Working strategically to shift thinking and activity for positive mental health outcomes will require loss and grief, death and **bereavement** personnel to adopt a wider view of their work, identifying in particular the role of policy in setting agendas for change and providing guidance for organizations. It also involves a focus on both prevention and intervention; that is, not only providing counselling but working strategically with schools to build their policies and practices to support grieving school community members. Adopting this approach has the potential to help all those affected by a loss, not just individuals identified as being at risk. By adopting this position, workers are more likely to ensure positive longer-term outcomes are achieved.

School communities, schooling and grief

Loss and grief and the aims of schooling

Throughout the last decade there has been increasing politicization of education. This has been fuelled by media stories, linked to society's increasing demand for accountability (both academically and socially) and situated within the context of a market economy. This creates pressures for school administrators in league table comparisons and in school governance decision making. The aims of schools in this sociopolitical context are seen to focus on guarding the 'reputation' of a school and maintaining or increasing enrolments.

In this context, an understanding of the place of personal and social aims of schools is important. Demands to meet these as well as academic aims have, in recent years, put additional pressure on schools. School staff are expected to perform a variety of different roles, not just as educators but as social workers and as a substitute for parents in developing values (Galloway 1990). In the management of grief in schools, this shift in expectations is articulated by teachers:

The surrogacy role of schools

When children's lives fall apart, often the family disintegrates. The only part of their life that will be constant is the school, so you need to have a routine and a process.

(Matt, headteacher for 10 years)

Yet there is a social work dimension to our role, which has always been there but is now much stronger and is part due to the problems in society. Somehow there is a surrogacy in our role in terms of presenting values to kids that used to come from parents in the home. It is not only a complementarity, sometimes WE are the ones giving the value base.

(Barney, headteacher for 1 year)

I think the role of schools has changed . . . Today in schools teachers have to do more. Because of changing families and unemployment, we have had to take on more roles and providing counselling and support for students is one of those. If we can provide it now we can prevent a lot of problems later.

(Guy, teacher for 9 years)

Some of the resistance from teachers to taking on these roles, or for the roles to be seen by parents as inappropriate, comes from the belief that human existence can be segmented and part of it left outside the classroom or school. This belief implies that the whole person comes together again when the teacher or student moves off the school site. It also relates to shifts in what is 'private' and only family business.

The impact of grief on young people and the ameliorative role, identified by research (Cutrona *et al.* 1990; Stroebe *et al.* 1993), of social support from individuals and the community (including the school community) points to a need for concern by all schools about this issue. The aims of schooling, though they differ in emphases, all indicate a school's responsibility in preparing young people for, and supporting them through, loss experiences. The experience of loss as a justification for attention by the school has been echoed by many writers (LaGrande 1988; Wass *et al.* 1990), its purpose being seen as 'enhancing human development and quality of life' (Weekes and Johnson 1992: 220). The challenges to adolescents' assumptive worlds (Janoff-Bulman 1989) provoked by loss events point to the supportive role of school staff in assisting students to gain and sustain a benevolent world view.

Why school communities?

A frame of reference that re-focuses the management of grief from individuals to encompass school communities extends the range of people who need to be included and attends to the school as a 'place', acknowledging the range of factors that can impact on individual and school loss experiences. School community members are diverse and each school community is a unique entity with a history, particular values and patterns of interaction. This broader perspective expands the traditional focus of individual one-to-one counselling and support encounters to include classroom learning and interactions of school community members, such as parents, teachers, administrative staff, members of governing bodies, local health and welfare agencies, as well as former students and staff. It also acknowledges the school as a setting with policies and practices that provide security, boundaries and connectedness and, in times of emotional upheaval, comfort and healing. The 'normality' of the school routine establishes these conditions. The normality does not simply transfer into 'business as usual' in times of crisis, but uses the structures of a school comprising the personal interactions, time schedules and pastoral care networks as a framework for effective management. The schools are also workplaces and important social institutions in parents' lives, as the chapters in this book will show.

This description of a school community includes **outside service providers**. The school can offer a healing environment and supportive interactions but, where there is widespread impact and/or traumatic reactions, the support of outside personnel with specialized knowledge of trauma and its manifestation is essential. Ideally, these personnel will have had previous formal work connections with schools.

This approach emphasizes the role of the school as a social institution because young people look to peers and teachers to help define the reality of their loss, express feelings associated with it, provide support and access to information, and integrate the experience into their lives. The school is not only a social institution for young people, but also a workplace for staff, all of whom spend many hours there. It can provide staff with an environment (in terms of policies, programmes and practices) that is supportive as well as access to individuals who can offer help through formal and informal mechanisms. But adopting this perspective on schooling and school communities will involve changes in the beliefs about the aims of schools, the professional roles of the teachers, and school policies and structures. An awareness of the extensive body of educational research literature about change and innovation (Hargreaves *et al.* 1998) is essential for policy makers in the mental health and loss and grief fields as well as educational decision makers.

The health promoting school

Two frameworks provide a structure for schools to establish a supportive environment for grief and locate loss and grief in a wider mental health promotion framework (Rowling 2000). These are the health promoting school framework (National Health and Medical Research Council 1996) and the World Health Organization model (Hendren *et al.* 1994) of comprehensive school-based mental health promotion.

The health promoting school framework (National Health and Medical Research Council 1996) is a modified version of the European model (Weare 2000). It is an approach to health issues advocated by the World Health Organization that is being adopted globally. A comprehensive approach to all health issues in schools involves having a sequential curriculum: the provision of training for teachers and active participation in learning by students. This curriculum is linked to the organizational structures and processes of the school environment that demonstrate the school's ethos. Schools need well-developed partnerships with parents and service providers to be able to address issues effectively. Figure 1.1 demonstrates how the framework can be applied to loss and grief.

A model of school-based mental health promotion

The second framework is adapted from a World Health Organization model (Hendren *et al.* 1994, Figure 1.2). Its key contribution is that it establishes a reasonable role for teachers and school communities and identifies the role of outside agencies. One block to the acceptance of grief as a school responsibility is that teachers feel ill-equipped. They believe that what is being expected of them is to be psychologists and social workers. But this framework locates their role within the entire school community (Sheehan *et al.* 2000), which for many is similar to their pastoral care work.

The top layer of activity exemplifies a 'population health' approach, in which there is consideration of the needs and goals of population groups in the community, and an awareness of the conditions of individuals that enhance or impede their health or the health of the community. Suicide and loss and grief (with the concomitant potential for negative mental health outcomes) are the concern of public health professionals in many countries (Hendren *et al.* 1994). The global concern and the variety of factors that contribute to this public health issue mean that a public health planning approach should be used to address the issues.

Loss and grief in this framework (Figure 1.3) means effort is placed on helping a large proportion of the population in a variety of ways. This involves **critical incident management plans**, pastoral care structures and links with outside agencies. This is in contrast to a targeted intervention for young people 'at risk'.

A second layer of activity is implementation of the curriculum for all students, but requiring only the involvement of those teachers who are trained and feel comfortable and supported in their role. Within this

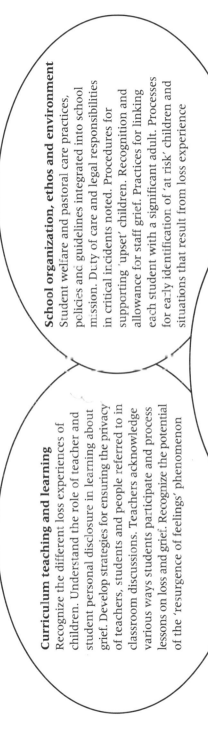

Curriculum teaching and learning
Recognize the different loss experiences of children. Understand the role of teacher and student personal disclosure in learning about grief. Develop strategies for ensuring the privacy of teachers, students and people referred to in classroom discussions. Teachers acknowledge various ways students participate and process lessons on loss and grief. Recognize the potential of the 'resurgence of feelings' phenomenon

School organization, ethos and environment
Student welfare and pastoral care practices, policies and guidelines integrated into school mission. Duty of care and legal responsibilities in critical incidents noted. Procedures for supporting 'upset' children. Recognition and allowance for staff grief. Practices for linking each student with a significant adult. Processes for early identification of 'at risk' children and situations that result from loss experience

Partnerships and services
Working relationships developed with local police. Collaborative practices between school and parents to support grieving students. Identify local community members who are trained in debriefing. Procedures developed with local agencies. Working relationships developed with local religious leaders. Invite Indigenous leaders and members of ethnic communities to school to talk about grieving practices

Figure 1.1 Loss and grief in the health promoting school framework (Rowling 2000).

Who is involved   **Level of intervention**

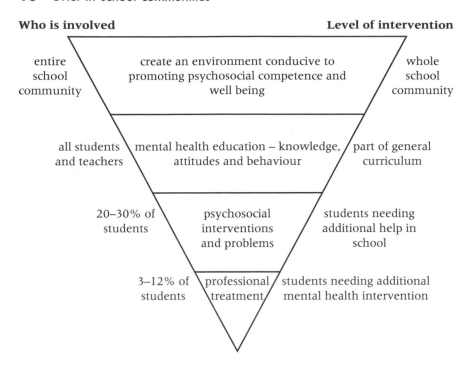

Figure 1.2 World Health Organization model of school-based mental health promotion.

model, about 20–30 per cent of students may need some additional help from support groups in the school or from outside agencies, for example those who are experiencing ongoing conflict between divorcing parents. Finally, some will need specialized interventions, such as refugee children, **Indigenous** youth or those who have been traumatized after witnessing a violent death.

Including loss and grief within the wider picture of mental health in schools helps to counter resistance from school personnel. It does not ask them to be social workers, but locates their current practice in a hierarchy of interventions, identifying a clear role for, and the potential contribution of, specialized helpers.

Research indicates that, next to personal resources, a major factor that influences the outcome of grieving for young people is the support they receive from adults and their peers (LaGrande 1988). This support needs to be provided in the range of ways identified in this mental health promotion framework.

Additionally, loss experiences have the capacity to affect teachers' workplace performance (Rowling 1995). This is a particular problem when the loss is a 'professional loss', directly related to the work envir-

Who is involved   Level of intervention

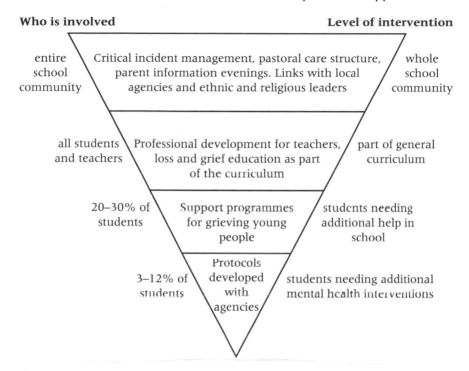

entire school community — Critical incident management, pastoral care structure, parent information evenings. Links with local agencies and ethnic and religious leaders — whole school community

all students and teachers — Professional development for teachers, loss and grief education as part of the curriculum — part of general curriculum

20–30% of students — Support programmes for grieving young people — students needing additional help in school

3–12% of students — Protocols developed with agencies — students needing additional mental health interventions

Figure 1.3 Loss and grief in a school-based mental health promotion framework.

onment, such as the death of a student or colleague, or a major accident or public crisis involving school personnel or property. This is described in more detail in Chapter 11. When discussing these issues, teachers often ask, 'What about us?' The comprehensive approach proposed provides for teachers' varying needs. It establishes a role for school communities as social systems that have the capacity to support members and to meet the needs of teachers, parents and students in a proactive way.

Loss and grief as a sensitive issue

School communities encounter debate and disagreement in attempts to change school practice regarding sensitive issues such as loss, death and suicide. There is a need to delineate the elements that create the sensitivity to plan for effective handling of the issues and thereby minimize negative outcomes (Rowling 1994). Schools are currently called upon to manage a range of these issues, including drug-use, HIV/AIDS, loss and grief, sexuality and violence in schools. An understanding of what creates this sensitivity, including the political, social and cultural contexts within which the issues arise, is necessary. Developing an awareness of these influences will provide guidance that enables the establishment of intervention strategies that facilitate the development of a comprehensive proactive approach to such issues in schools, thereby enabling educational institutions to fulfil legal and moral responsibilities for school community members.

Literature on personal and social education, health education, life skills education, and loss and grief research contains no adequate documentation that explicates the nature of sensitive issues in schools. Passing references are made, such as 'the issue needs to be handled sensitively' or 'care needs to be taken with sensitive issues like contraception, abortion, homosexuality and masturbation'. What makes an issue sensitive in the school context? An examination of the issues considered to be sensitive, such as drug use, sexuality and sexual abuse (Rowling 1994), reveals that the basis of the sensitivity can be:

- the emotionality of the issue, such as embarrassment, distress and questions of privacy;
- the involvement of the individual, including their inner thoughts, behaviours and sense of self;
- the existence of intense and deeply felt personal reactions in parents, young people, teachers and in the wider community;
- the particular social context; and
- the meanings issues have for individuals, as determined by wider political and cultural factors, gender, religious beliefs and personal experiences.

The emotional reactions are a result of the interaction of the issue, a person's beliefs and experiences, the context and the meaning of the issues to the individual (Figure 1.4). In the school setting, this emotional

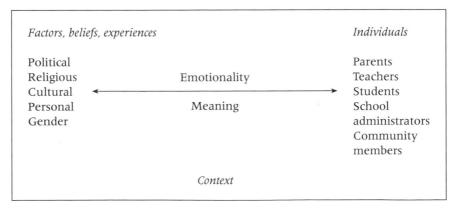

Figure 1.4 A model of elements in sensitive issues.

interaction can lead to 'knee-jerk' reactions. Consequently, schools need to be proactive, as these reactions have the potential for enormous individual and school community harm. Although a key element is the *individual*, the meanings are given a sensitive focus by the context.

Current approaches to loss and grief

In a recent study in England, Bullivant (1998) found that most local education authorities have no policy relating to bereavement and traumatic incidents. This finding is supported by a cross-cultural study of a sample of schools in England and Australia (Rowling and Holland 2000), which found that 94 per cent of an Australian sample of 145 schools had such plans in place, compared with only 15 per cent of an English sample of 200 schools. The researchers suggested that the difference was due to the differing policy contexts for grief, and the lack of teacher training and minimal education about grief in England. Rowling and Holland concluded that a more comprehensive approach would be achieved only when there was system level policy and training support, as well as school community and individual teacher recognition of their potential contribution to young people's well-being.

Consider the following events, all of which are incidents I have encountered:

- A teacher Jim has to explain to his class a student's absence. Her father, who was the school janitor, had died suddenly the day before of a heart attack.
- The school psychologist Pat has talked in the previous two weeks with five children who are showing behaviour problems. All of them have parents who have separated in the previous 12 months.
- Aziz's mother tells the deputy head, Bernadette, that her husband is dying of cancer. Aziz says that he does not want anyone else in the school to know.
- Tony is coping with the death of a younger sibling after a long illness.
- The headteacher Jeff is faced with the suicide at school of Sandra, a senior prefect who was found dead from an overdose in the school toilets by her pastoral care teacher Denise.
- John approaches his colleague Marianne for advice on how to talk to his fellow teacher Steve who is returning to school after the death of his father.

These circumstances could all be viewed from an individual perspective: some people need support; some people need individual or group counselling; others need information through **professional development**.

They illustrate the varying needs of school community members and the depth and variety of grief issues that schools encounter. The health promoting school framework (Figure 1.1), which identifies the elements of a comprehensive approach (Rowling 2000), provides for this depth and variety. It would involve the following.

First, it would require a curriculum that is proactive – that is, loss experiences need to be included as a part of existing personal and social and life skills programmes, not just included after a crisis has occurred. This approach facilitates the normalization of grief through education (Zisook 1987). The orientation of this curriculum would not just involve understanding feelings and reactions as in past curriculum approaches, but the teaching of skills to enable individuals to cope and to be supportive to others (Glassock and Rowling 1992; Rowling 2000). Training of teachers to handle this issue and the use of the active learning and teaching styles may be necessary. The training needs to involve both cognitive and emotional aspects as well as pedagogical skills (see Chapter 12 for more detail).

Second, a holistic approach to loss and grief would involve the organization, ethos and environment of the school. The ethos of a supportive context would include: the policies of the school that provide for the emotional welfare of students; a well-developed pastoral care system; clear procedures for referral of students to outside agencies; availability of a school-based counselling service; and a peer support programme. It would also include staff relationships: how the school cares for its staff; the involvement of teachers in the development of policies and procedures; and the relationships between the **headteacher** and individual staff members. These components create the ethos of the school as a caring environment. The ethos is part of the 'hidden curriculum', so it may mean making the belief system that is the basis of a supportive environment explicit. As described earlier, sensitive issues have characteristics that are more concerned with the personal and social aims of schools. These characteristics, including emotionality, values and the role of the individual, mean that the caring ethos of the school as an organization, which purports to be concerned about the school community's well-being, will be represented by the existence and implementation of policies for handling sensitive issues (Rowling 1996a) and the leadership of the school. For example, a critical incident management plan and its active support by a headteacher demonstrates the organization's commitment to the well-being of school community members if a traumatic incident occurs.

Third, partnerships and services should include inter-agency collaboration for referral for mental health problems, such as for staff traumatized by violence from students, and the involvement of outside bereavement support agencies, police and community health and social services in the planning and delivery of policies and programmes such as critical incident management. Also included is parent–school liaison: curriculum consultation about loss and grief; the implementation of a critical incident management plan; and teacher–parent communication about grieving adolescents. Another aspect of the community outreach could be training for family and friends. This training has been advocated as a way to help such individuals accept the expression of feelings, gain insight into their own grief and help them support grieving family members (Zisook 1987).

Particular processes and practices need to connect these areas, as they are not discrete entities. Consultation and information exchange are vital components of developing a comprehensive approach to grief. Building on existing activities, identifying gaps and planning school-determined procedures are elements of exemplary practice.

The gaps identified by research in the handling of loss and grief in schools suggest that it is not currently an integral part of school community practice. The holistic approach advocated above is innovative. Yet some schools do recognize this need:

School acceptance of a comprehensive approach

The school community is in a state of bereavement. I think the management of it has got to be the school because the children's eyes will focus on the staff in the school and the parents will focus on the staff in the school. But I really think that no matter how well schools are equipped to deal, they should not do it on their own. Other people need to do lots of other things to allow you to get the school back on course.

(Brian, headteacher for 9 years)

I feel that where you need to deal with these issues is in the community that went through it with you. I feel that that is part of our role as a school.

(Lily, headteacher for 5 years)

I think the strength of this school at being able to deal with incidents is that the students certainly have felt, and the staff certainly have felt, part of that community and responsibility for each other in their community. That has helped us greatly to deal with incidents.

(Lucas, headteacher for 2 years)

Other teachers have talked about former students, even 'fringe' students, coming back to the school to sign condolence cards, demonstrating a two-way process of the school providing the opportunity and the students feeling comfortable in taking it up. Another example of the 'extended community' of a school was of a postman who heard accounts on his round of a student who had died in traumatic circumstances. He too sought help in the school:

He came in and said, 'Is there someone here I can talk to, I am really having a hard time dealing with it?'

(Fred, headteacher for 1 year)

Conclusion

The frameworks for mental health promotion, understanding sensitive issues and the health promoting school provide valuable guidance for schools to approach loss and grief (Rowling 2000). They link with the recommendations from the research literature on social support (Cutrona *et al.* 1990), which indicates that there are different forms of support, such as informational support, emotional support and network support, which can come from different sources

This comprehensive approach is not without controversy, for example the debate over the school's role and a parent's role. Developing a whole-school approach to loss and grief can serve to intervene, to manage critical incidents and to support grieving young people. It can also act in a preventive way through information exchange and positive attitude formation about help seeking, help receiving and supporting others when the need arises. Acknowledging the impact of loss on school community members indicates a school's aim to provide a safe and supportive environment. This chapter argues for the need to place this in a wider mental health promotion framework. This proactive approach demonstrates a caring ethos for individuals and establishes caring as normative behaviour with its potential positive mental health outcome of connectedness to school (Rutter 1995). In accepting grief as part of young people's lives, school communities will have to be proactive in plans to help them adapt to these life events. This is the only way school communities will truly support young people.

This 'new' public health approach to loss and grief is justifiable given the potential negative mental health outcomes of traumatic events (Yule 1989) and loss experiences (Raphael 1985) and the impact of these on population health outcomes. A proactive approach also contributes to the school being seen to act prudently by staff, students, parents and the wider community.

A violent rape and murder of a student highlights the complexity of issues a school faces. The range of issues that will be explored in subsequent chapters are: the need for information exchange between school and agencies such as the police; school personnel being informed and having a plan; the criticism of the management of a crisis; the community's concerns; the short- and long-term impact on the school; the experience of teachers; the reactions of students; and the importance of 'caring' for all students and staff.

Harry, a teacher for 14 years, recounts the experience:

A school's experience

*I was the **year adviser** when, Maxine, a girl in my year was murdered. On Monday I heard it on the news when I was driving to school. Her name wasn't mentioned. We found it was one of our students. That was a real crisis in the school. . . . At the time we didn't have any sort of plan of action on how to deal with this. In hindsight we would have done things differently. But it was a major crisis within the school. It did affect the tone of the school for the rest of the year. It certainly disrupted the school. One of the unfortunate things was that she was no angel. In fact, she was in a peer group of girls in year 9, the typical year 9 that fester and infect everybody else, cause trouble, bitchiness and backbiting, rumour spreading and violence. You know that scenario? That core group was devastated. They were going after anyone who said anything about her. There was this terrible 'to do' with some other girls in year 9. The comment was made, 'I am glad she is dead'. It was one particular girl who had been accused of this, a meek mild, quiet, very passive kid. She was accused of saying this. There were fist fights and police were called. There was a real problem of what to do, how to judge the parameters, how long are you supposed to be sympathetic? Staff coming to you 6 weeks down the track, and saying: 'This kid is still. . . . they are using this, they are using this to get out of class, they are using this as an excuse'. There is obviously a socially acceptable time that you grieve and after that you are right. Oh, it was very messy. There was a fair amount of public outcry within the community as well. We had to sort of keep a lid on the whole thing because each day you wouldn't know what would happen. I found it was a very difficult time dealing with each day. It was interesting actually, there was no recognition given to the teachers' need for support. We only got the formalized support from the headteacher.*

Implications for practice

- Deal with grief within the social context of the school: its people, structures, processes and policies.
- Develop a framework that will help to provide sustainable links with community agencies.
- A comprehensive approach involving all school community members will be most effective in achieving positive outcomes.
- There are benefits in considering loss and grief within the wider mental health promotion, suicide and public health fields.

Further reading

Galloway, D. (1990) *Pupil Welfare and Counselling: An Approach to Personal and Social Education across the Curriculum.* London: Longman.

Rowling, L. (2000) *MindMatters: A Whole School Approach to Loss and Grief.* Canberra: Mental Health Promotion Branch, Commonwealth Department of Health and Aged Care (available at http://www.curriculum.edu.au/mindmatters).

Rowling, L. and Holland, J. (2000) Grief and school communities: the impact of social context, a comparison between Australia and England, *Death Studies,* 24(1): 15–24.

Sheehan, M., Marshall, B., Cahill, H., Rowling, L. and Holdsworth, R. (2000) *SchoolMatters: Mapping and Managing Mental Health in Schools.* Canberra: Commonwealth Department of Health and Aged Care (available at http://www.curriculum.edu.au/mindmatters).

CHAPTER 2

Impact of loss on children and adolescents

Introduction

This chapter reviews briefly information about young people's understanding about loss, factors that influence their loss, reactions and adapting strategies and identifies approaches to supporting them. The intention is not to reiterate the depth of information covered in other texts, but rather to present background information for those new to the field. Silverman (2000: 45) warns, 'Children are not their stages of development'. This statement cautions us to keep young people as the focus of our attention in understanding and supporting them in their grief, not to pigeonhole them according to their developmental age. With this caveat in mind, developmental age is used in this chapter as the 'organizing' structure in a descriptive rather than prescriptive way in preference to chronological age. It is also important to observe young people's reactions, listen to their concerns and the way they view and interpret them (Barnard *et al.* 1999).

Cognitive, emotional and social development all influence children's and adolescents' understanding of loss and their grief reactions. Additionally, it is the interaction of young people with the events they experience and with their environment, particularly the adults in that environment, that is important. In indicating guidelines of what may be supportive for grieving young people, the underpinning perspective adopted is to view loss experiences as not just having negative outcomes but as having maturational influences.

Loss experiences of young people

Loss is the state of being deprived of someone or something valued (Howarth and Leaman 2001). For young people, it is also associated with loss of safety and familiarity as well as emotional connections. The loss events most commonly considered with young people are family deaths and divorce, with their accompanying emotional, cognitive and behavioural responses. There are, however, other more frequent loss experiences that young people encounter. These include: a change of school, neighbourhood or migration to a new country; the loss of health through illness or accident; the loss of expectation, such as failing to make a team; the death of a beloved pet; the loss of self-esteem through a friend's rejection or a failure in school; a broken love relationship; and the passage from one life stage to another. Reactions to these losses will vary according to the nature of the loss itself, the personal circumstances and characteristics of the individual, the reactions of adults and the amount and type of support that is available. For example, the loss of a sibling is quite different from the loss of a parent (Worden 1996; Davies 1999).

As indicated in Chapter 1, parents can no longer maintain an innocence about death in children. Although there are limitations to young children's understanding, they do understand some aspects of loss; they certainly do feel it and do take action to cope. Barnard *et al.* (1999) maintain that, with appropriate knowledge and support, young people have the capacity to be resilient to loss experiences. Being resilient does not mean they are not affected, but that, with support, they have the capacity to bounce back. Their attempts to manage the stress associated with these events, however, may not be recognized by adults and opportunities to explore their feelings and concerns and alter misperceptions may be lost. These misperceptions occur because children's understanding does not progress in an orderly manner as if through 'stages' (Silverman 2000), although this is a common portrayal of the development of understanding. For example, 13-year-olds may show vestiges of magical thinking, believing they have super power that can make things happen, when faced with a traumatic loss, even though they have well-developed concepts about other aspects of the loss. Adults may believe the magical thinking denotes a less well-developed concept of death and, consequently, limit explanations. As stressed earlier in this chapter, while stage of cognitive development is important in identifying levels of understanding, experiences of loss are also critical factors. The following guidelines indicate what could be expected of young people at different ages, but understanding and reactions need to be viewed as elements of a process (Silverman 2000).

Preschool to kindergarten

Concept of death and loss

Research that helps delineate cognitive developmental understandings about death helps to identify shifts in children's comprehension about death and loss. Four areas have been identified as being important: universality (inevitability), irreversibility (finality), non-functionality (cessation of bodily processes) and causality (objective causes) (Deveau 1995). Research in the last decade or two has questioned earlier findings about at what age all these understandings of a mature concept of death occur. This developing understanding has been compounded by advances in medical technology (Deveau 1995). In assessing children's understanding of death, it is important to take into account the events young people have experienced, their interaction with adults and the wider culture and exposure to losses. All these factors influence children's developing concepts in each of these four areas.

From a school perspective, preschoolers are likely to be the youngest children teachers encounter. Children of this age have difficulty assuming the viewpoint of another, as the world is seen to revolve around them. Their magical thinking may result in them feeling responsible in some way if a parent dies or their parents separate. Children of this age believe that their feelings are shared by others and that things are as they appear and will remain this way. Life is the experience of movement and so all things that move, live. The absence of movement can denote 'non-aliveness'. If a death occurs in the family, preschoolers may focus on daily living requirements rather than the death itself. Death is not seen as final, but as being similar to sleep. Factual explanations in physical and biological terms are developmentally appropriate. The 'why' of death is better explained as part of the natural order of things – beginnings and endings – rather than in philosophical and religious terms. Children will make literal interpretations of explanations, so with religious interpretations heaven is a place that they can go and visit for the day and God is a person that they can all go and stay with. The use of developmentally appropriate language and concepts can help to modify these interpretations.

Reactions and adapting

For preschoolers, their reactions may be intense but of short duration and can fluctuate between grieving and normal behaviour, 'dosing' as a way of managing overwhelming emotions. They are unlikely to be able to explain how they are feeling. Adults will need to observe their social interactions to assess the impact of the loss. Under stress, preschoolers may lose their most recently acquired skills, with grief being expressed in regressive behaviours, bedwetting, tantrums and changes in eating and sleeping patterns. Adults may misinterpret children's reactions, with no reaction (no crying, child continues to play) being viewed as the child's non-experience of grief, when in reality the child may be depressed and withdrawn. Young children use distraction to adapt familiar activities and routines, denial and fantasy.

How teachers and care-givers can help

Teachers and care-givers assist preschoolers by leading them towards the understandings of older children. This can be achieved by developing their understanding that with death life stops as far as the physical body is concerned, the deceased cannot return and the body is buried. The concepts of universality and non-functionality are most likely to be progressively understood by preschoolers. Reassurance is needed about the continuation of their daily living requirements, such as eating, sleeping and the presence of care-givers. Joshua, a headteacher, reported the reactions of young children to a bomb scare on the third day of a new school year: 'My new toy story lunch box is going to get blown up!' and 'They are after my HOUSE!' He commented on the need to take these fears seriously, even though some teachers saw them as trivial.

Early primary

Concept of death and loss

Universality is most commonly understood before irreversibility and non-functionality. Causality is the most complex understanding (Deveau 1995). Hence in this age group children can accept that people die, but may externalize it as 'bogeymen' or 'ghost-like figures' and take actions such as chanting spells to avoid it. They can be fearful of the rituals and symbols of death. They progress from this interest in graves and funerals to an interest in what happens after death. If children have some religious education, they may have some idea of a soul. However, at the time of a death, children are more likely to need reassurances about life than religious explanations. From a psychosocial viewpoint, they have a greater capacity to take the perspective of others and can be conscious of the injustice of events. In the case of parental separation, they can understand that parental conflicts are separate from them, but their self-image is still dependent on their view of their parents and how others see their parents.

Reactions and adapting

When involved in traumatic events, children of early primary age can revert to clinging and disobedient behaviours. They can be sad and depressed and immobilized by these feelings (Johnson 1993). Emotional needs may be translated into hunger for food and material things. Physical reactions occur. Although headaches and stomach aches may be linked by adults to grief, other physical reactions, such as sighing, feeling 'lousy', feeling hollow and vacant, uncontrollable shaking, proneness to accidents and over-sensitivity to stimuli, may not be perceived as reactions to the loss experience. Younger children do not know for certain that life will continue, only adults have this knowledge.

How teachers and care-givers can help

It is important, then, for teachers and parents to pay attention to a young person's reality and adopt a flexible perspective when assessing their understanding. Clear descriptions of what can be expected in funerals and other rituals help to dispel fears. It is essential that school staff are sensitive to the impact of the stresses from these life events, with the potential for falling behind in schoolwork. Early intervention to maintain success in learning bolsters the self-esteem that has been undermined by the loss experiences. When a peer has died, using creative approaches that facilitate grieving is helpful, particularly non-verbal approaches for younger children and boys. Equally important is allowing those who are not experiencing the reactions of their peers the permission not to grieve.

Late primary

Concept of death and loss

The most important shift for pre-adolescents is in conceptual development. With an increased ability to think abstractly, they have a greater capacity to understand the rituals and practicalities surrounding death, such as burial requirements. Their questions and comments can be gruesome and sickening to some adults. They can reason sequentially and understand cause-and-effect relationships (Silverman 2000). There is also a developing sense of independence, with a growing importance being given to those outside the family. The loss of a best friend through death or a move to another school can be strongly felt. The cognitive ability to compare family life before parental divorce with the experience of current family life, with perhaps a drop in family income and a move to a less desirable neighbourhood, can be sources of shame and anger.

Reactions and adapting

The experience of a traumatic event can stimulate mature or regressive behaviour. Uncertain about how exactly to react, pre-adolescents need cues and explanations about how to act. Social withdrawal is a common sign of fear and worry (Worden 1996). Their feelings of helplessness can turn to anger, with fighting and opposition to authority figures, or they may become the class clown. This helps prevent them from feeling unhappy and emotionally vulnerable. Some use elaborate defences such as denying feelings and discussing upsetting events in a completely unemotional way. There may be grief without tears.

How teachers and care-givers can help

Although they are able to understand more, late primary school age children may not be able to deal emotionally with everything they experience. Drama is a useful strategy for exploring feelings and behaviours without the personal disclosure feared by developing adolescents. Some groups are more ready to plan and conduct class ceremonies of remembrance if a classmate has died. Groups within a class may create a scrapbook of their peer's work, certificates and photographs and give it to their classmate's family. Being outside and involved in activities that do not require much concentration, such as hiking and swimming, can help relieve tension, especially for boys. Care-givers may need to judge current behaviour against responses in the past. Reassurance that their feelings are acceptable and support by answering questions will help even if information is not sought openly by the young people. Reasonable restraint still may need to be placed on behaviour that is hurting others and themselves. Maintaining a sense of community in the classroom and the school was found to assist late primary school students with the death of classmates in a school bus accident (Toubiana et al. 1988, cited in Ringler and Hayden 2000).

Early secondary school

One of the many feelings grieving people experience is a loss of control over events. Young people in particular can be affected by these feelings because they are concomitantly experiencing a loss of control in relation to their body shape. Puberty, with all its accompanying physical changes, makes them feel that many things are out of their control. Psychologically, the developing identity of a young person can be threatened by the death of a parent or parental separation; their security is disturbed because the concept of 'the family' changes and their assumptions about the world are challenged. The first broken love affair can have a major impact on adolescents' views of themselves. Social support has been found to be a moderator for adolescents' loss (Balk 1983; Gray 1989). The role of bereavement support groups linked to schools is explored in Chapter 9.

Concept of death and loss

Early adolescents are able to think hypothetically and deductively and understand the perspective of others (Silverman 2000). They are aware of the personal and social implications of loss experiences, for example the separation of their parents and being 'different'. This behaviour is shaped by the real action of others and the sanctioning this does or does not provide. A 13-year-old, Earl, in discussing the death of his uncle, reported the teasing that he witnessed his friend experiencing:

> His Dad died of cancer and he had a few weeks off. Then he came back to school and this older kid gave him some crap about it. He went off crying. You are better leaving them alone when that happens. It is not good standing there watching them crying making them think 'Oh God I'm a wimp!' So I kept quiet [about the death of his uncle].

It was the teasing that Earl had observed and the lack of support from other students that silenced him.

Reactions and adapting

The developmental changes during adolescence put young persons particularly at risk. Their emotional reactions are characterized by 'highs' and 'lows' due to changing hormone concentrations. Loss experiences can intensify emotional responses. Bereaved adolescents are more likely to have less self-esteem, exhibit more withdrawn and anxious behaviour, and experience more health problems and greater depression than bereaved pre-adolescents (Worden 1996). Cognitively, adolescents' developing assumptions about the world: its benevolence, meaningfulness and the worthiness of themselves (Schwartberg and Janoff-Bulman 1991) are affected by loss experiences.

Of significant concern for school staff is that loss experiences are associated with poor educational outcomes (Corr and Balk 1996). Grief takes energy and attention, the effects of which can be seen in particular in areas that require cognitive problem solving (Stevenson 1996). Although this is the case at all ages, it is particularly prevalent among secondary school students. Students can lack motivation and the ability to concentrate. In addition, increased absenteeism is possible. Conversely, a smaller number of students can immerse themselves in schoolwork and extra-curricula activities. Teachers need to be aware that this may be protective in the short term, but school performance can then drop months after the event. Responses to trauma include appetite disorders and maladaptive responses, such as substance abuse and promiscuous behaviour (Johnson 1993). Often lost for words, early adolescents may use metaphors to describe their feelings. Jock said that his grief was 'like a live wire through his body, giving him shocks at unexpected times'. Denial and avoidance are adaptive mechanisms that adolescents use because of fear of losing control. Anger can give a sense of control that counteracts the helplessness. They are over-concerned about the acceptability of their responses by their peers. Physical activity is a commonly used adaptive strategy.

One of the important outcomes of loss experiences for young people is personal growth. This supports the importance of loss and grief as a focus in mental health promotion detailed in Chapter 1. John, a 13-year-old, demonstrated great maturity as a result of contending with the terminal illness of his mother. She had been very ill for several years and was being given pain-killing drugs that caused epileptic attacks. John felt he was different from his friends because he had to account continually for his whereabouts in case his mother had a turn. He had a younger sister and felt a great deal of responsibility for her as well as his mother. John's descriptions of his reactions to his mother's illness seemed to minimize the impact of it on him, but periodically his outbursts of anger at school led to fights. His recounting of a nightmare indicates underlying concerns:

John: *It does get a bit difficult. School is mostly the only time I do get to have time with my friends.*

Louise: *Why is that?*

John: *Because I am the eldest in the family, I have to stay home and look after Mum most of the time, in case anything happens. Because Mum has epileptic fits, she gets dehydrated very easily.*

Louise: *Have you had to manage your Mum's fits?*

John: *Yeah. I just talk to her and try to get her around, yell at my sister to go next door and get the next door neighbour. She just sits there crying. Mum has had two fits when I have been around. Because of that I do get worried and half the time, when she does have them, I am by myself with my sister and no-one is really around to help.*

Louise: *So you feel it is all your responsibility? And what if she might die if you don't do something?*

John: *Yeah. [Pause] . . . Like she's told me WHAT [John's emphasis] to do when she has them and I know WHAT TO DO [John's empha-*

*sis] but I am afraid something might go wrong, something I don't
know about.*

Louise: *Sometimes people of your age dream a lot. Have you had any
dreams, good dreams or bad dreams?*

John: *I have dreams, mostly nightmares.*

Louise: *What is happening in them?*

John: *[Pause] . . . Mostly my sister getting kidnapped.*

Louise: *Oh!*

John: *And we never find her and [in the nightmare] Mum is always
upset about that.*

John appeared mature and able to cope but his nightmares revealed his
continuing fears. Young people who experience nightmares and hallucina-
tions can be very frightened by them, fearing they are going mad.

How teachers and care-givers can help

Comparing current actions of students against behaviour exhibited
before their loss is one way for adults to assess difficulty in adapting,
although grieving behaviour can be intense. This is likely to decrease
slowly with time. Despite the appearance of maturity in understanding
events and the possible access to more personal adaptive mechanisms,
reassurance from adults, such as 'It is okay to be angry', is still needed.
If a peer has died, some students may want to attend the funeral and
write notes, poems and in other ways memorialize their schoolmate.
Teachers need to guide and be guided by their class in these activities. If
an individual student has experienced a loss, they can be helped if too
upset to remain in a lesson by being given a pass to go and talk with
someone. To help the student regain a sense of control, they should be
encouraged to nominate the pre-arranged person, who can be anyone
from the school psychologist to the headteacher, librarian or even the
janitor, whoever the student feels comfortable with.

Late secondary school

Concept of death and loss

Older adolescents, who are more able to contemplate the way the world
is, are more focused on creating 'meaning' out of their loss. They face
the dual challenges of fear of loss of control and struggles with their
emerging independence. If the death is that of a parent, it can challenge
this growth of independence. There can be a sense of abandonment by
adults if a parent dies. This was a feeling expressed by Gary, whom the

author talked with over a period of two years (Rowling 1994). Just before his father died, 17-year-old Gary had obtained his driver's licence (a rite of passage for young males). His father helped him buy an old car. The car needed work but his father was too ill to help. Gary was not able to do it alone. In describing how worthless he was feeling after his father's death because he was not able to work on the car as his father wanted, he also indicated how directionless the death of his father made him feel:

> *This feeling began when I got the car and got worse when Dad died. The thoughts that go through my head are, 'Dad's not there. I am not worthwhile. I have nothing to follow, nothing to stand up to. My father was the authority, now I can't follow what he did'.*

The role of the interpersonal context to older adolescents in strengthening their self-image is particularly important. A broken love relationship can result not only in the loss of love and companionship, but also a loss of the sense of self created through that relationship. The impact of broken relationships, which result in multiple losses, is often minimized by adults or the impact may not be recognized at all.

The ability to speculate, to be reflective and philosophical about life and death is also present. Neroli, a 16-year-old, reported her reaction to an incident outside her school in which a car driven by a 17-year-old with four friends as passengers struck another group of students tossing them over and under the car (Rowling 1994). Neroli reports seeing the incident on the television:

> *I just couldn't believe it! I had just turned the television on to watch the news and I saw a friend who was close to me, in an accident. I was shocked! Something had happened to our school, our friends. We walked that way to our buses. It makes you wonder!*

Reactions and adapting

Texts frequently encourage an understanding of young people's reactions to loss through stage or phase categorization (for example Mallon 1998) with or without the warning of the individuality of grief. Problems can occur with this stage approach and its step-like progression if the individuality of grief is underestimated. This focus on emotional responses and the suggestion of some linear model of responses misrepresents young people's experiences. For example, the index entry for 'reaction to grief and loss' in the book *Working with Children in Grief and Loss* (Lindsay and Elsegood 1996: 210) is 'see emotional responses'. Recent research indicates that this is a misinterpretation of their experience, particularly for young males (Rowling 2002). Although younger males might like to talk with friends, the 'telling' may not be about feelings. Older males may just want to be in the company of friends. Differences between the sexes and young people are discussed in more detail in Chapter 11. A subtle form of anger from adolescents can be in 'putting up a wall'. This helps keep people away and offers protection from further losses. One clue that this might be happening is when a young person withdraws from friendships and other close relationships. Older adolescents may try to cope and divert emotional pain by using drugs, driving cars fast or adopting promiscuous behaviour.

Gary, a 17-year-old, perceived his experience had contributed to his growth, prompting the development of insight into other people's feelings:

> It has affected me in the way I can read another person, like I sit back, look at them, look at the way they are behaving, what they say to people, sit back and think, 'You're not very secure in yourself'. I never say it. I keep it inside. But I understand how they are feeling.

How teachers and care-givers can help

Just as with younger adolescents, support actions need to focus on increasing and maintaining older adolescents' sense of control, either as a group or individually, depending on the circumstances. A right to privacy and being alone should be respected. Flexibility with school attendance and required tasks can be valuable. For example, the student could work alone in the library for some of the school day as a way of easing them back into full-time classroom attendance. The use of humour as a cognitive adaptive strategy, often used by this group, is often misunderstood. It relieves tension, can help stimulate memories and divert experiencing the pain (Martin and Doka 2000). However, for some people, joking demonstrates insensitivity so that the positive benefits are lost. Teachers in a school where there had been an accident were horrified the next day to hear senior boys making jokes about it (Rowling 1994). Adolescents may need to be helped to recognize in what circumstances it is appropriate to use humour.

The provision of honest factual information to support and expand the cognitive development of older adolescents is essential. This can enable the assumption of adult behaviours and responsibilities (Tyson-Rawson 1996). Assumptive worlds change with a greater perception of the randomness of events in life and an increased sense of responsibility and less control in one's life (Tyson-Rawson 1996). Adolescents who experienced less emotional distress were found to do so when they were able to satisfactorily incorporate their experiences, with the assistance of peers and supportive adults, into their assumptions about the world (Schwartberg and Janoff-Bulman 1991). Many of the deaths young people experience are of their peers. These are often in traumatic circumstances, for example the death of a friend by suicide. Special help may be needed in these circumstances to enable the young person to overcome feelings of guilt ('if only I had') or anxiety ('will I do the same thing?'). Suicide is discussed in more detail in Chapter 10. They are also likely to be angrier than at a younger age, because of their developing understanding of the wider context in which their loss has occurred and the extent of the issues involved. Anger is likely to be expressed in more extreme and noticeable ways. Additionally, the failure of adults to recognize the multiple losses in the death of a peer or broken love relationship diminishes the young person's experience and increases their withdrawal rather than support seeking (Rowling 2002).

Conclusion

Grief is not limited to weeks and months. Young people and adolescents in particular re-evaluate earlier losses, developing new perspectives as they mature. In understanding young people's reactions to loss and adapting strategies, it is important to note that denial can appear at all ages. This may be a help or a hindrance. Additionally, as young people grow, new questions will arise about earlier losses. Both these factors provide the possibility for a later loss to produce grief that connects with a previous loss. When this occurs, some time may have passed since the loss and teachers, care-givers and other supportive adults may try to suppress these inquiries. The reoccurrence of grief does not necessarily indicate that the event has continued to have a negative impact on a young life, or that the experience has not been integrated into their life, rather that grief is an ongoing process of developing meaning about the loss and that new dimensions of the loss have been brought into awareness (Klass *et al.* 1996). For example, significant life transitions, such as graduation, can rekindle thoughts and feelings about the absence of a parent. This 'resurgence of feelings' phenomenon (Rowling 2000) can account for unexpected reactions. But it also offers opportunities to revisit and gain better understanding of previous losses.

Changes in young people's assumptive worlds, the development of new meanings about the world and their place in it are possible outcomes of loss experiences, outcomes that can be guided by supportive adults. The intensity of emotional responses, reconciling cognitive inconsistencies and in-depth exploration of hitherto unfamiliar concepts help young people to overcome a complex variety of developmental tasks. The potential for grief experiences to contribute to the development of greater maturity (Corr and Balk 1996) highlights the importance of support as a mental health promotion strategy.

Several themes have been interwoven in this chapter. The need to observe and listen to young people is central. The focus when helping young people should be on individuals or classes, with physical and psychosocial safety important aspects of a school's provision of care. For adolescents, respect and providing opportunities to increase and maintain personal control are essential support strategies. This assists them to make meaning out of their changing worlds, when assumptions about the nature of the world and how much control they can exert are being challenged. Young people grappling with these issues can experience a sense of personal development.

Implications for practice

- Observe young people's reactions and listen to their concerns.
- Strategies to support children and young people experiencing a loss should be considerate of their individual developmental stage.
- When significant life transitions occur, feelings can resurface from the past. Proactive responses to these will help to manage potentially problematic circumstances.

Further reading

Corr, C. and Balk, D. (eds) (1996) *Handbook of Adolescent Death and Bereavement*. New York: Springer.

Deveau, E.J. (1995) Perceptions of death through the eyes of children, in D.W. Adams and E.J. Deveau (eds) *Beyond the Innocence of Childhood: Factors Influencing Children's and Adolescent's Perceptions and Attitudes towards Death*, Vol. 1. New York: Baywood.

Silverman, P.R. (2000) *Never too Young to Know: Death in Children's Lives*. New York: Oxford University Press.

Tyson-Rawson, K.J. (1996) Adolescent responses to the death of a parent, in C.A. Corr and D.E. Balk (eds) *Handbook of Adolescent Death and Bereavement*. New York: Springer.

CHAPTER 3

Teachers – being human

Dunblane

The newspaper report said
that from the placement of the bodies
it looked as if she had been trying to
shield the children.

I can see her
arms spreadeagled
fear jumping up in her throat
as she pleaded for the
madness to stop,
her flesh and bone
not strong enough
to stop the bullets
from ripping and tearing
her wee ones' lives away.
She was one of us
a teacher doing her job
'duty of care' we call it.
We were all wounded
when the madman opened fire
                    Andrew Macfarlane

Introduction

The importance of the social context and leadership in school communities is highlighted when exploring teachers' attitudes to death and loss, their acceptance or rejection of the need to respond to critical incidents and support young people, and their preparedness to teach about loss. Leaman (1995: 32) presents a pessimistic view of the teacher in England 'as perhaps the very worst person to deal with issues connected with death'. He sees them as anxious when discussing death and as members of the middle class, disinclined to talk. His views would be challenged by many in the teaching profession, yet there is research evidence for this reluctance on the part of teachers. There is evidence to suggest that loss and grief create great anxiety for teachers in England (Bullivant 1998), anxiety that is greater than that experienced by teachers in Australia (Rowling and Holland 2000). Leaman (1995) explains this reluctance on the part of teachers in England to deal with issues connected to death as a clash of values in the interactions between students and teachers. This is a simplistic interpretation of a complex issue. It is my contention that the context is a significant contributing factor. This sociocultural, political and educational context can be influenced to be more supportive to teachers and the challenges they face. This will involve the need for a change, on the part of some teachers, in the conception of their role, from a teacher of subjects to a teacher of children, greater systemic support and professional development. There can be open or subtle resistance from teachers who are challenged by change when this shift is experienced.

This chapter details some of the challenges faced and the existing quality practice of teachers. Increasing their capacity to be supportive is essential. In the event of a critical incident, research evidence supports the crucial role of school personnel in returning a school to life before the trauma (Nader and Pynoos 1993). The extent to which they are able to achieve this is dependent on the distress they are experiencing and, as a sequela, the amount of support in any form they do or do not receive.

The teacher described in the poem introducing this chapter was exercising her 'duty of care'. This is a key concept in any discussion of supporting young people, not just a legal interpretation but a moral, educational and societal responsibility. The duty of care owed by staff to children is that of a reasonable parent and professional and will be governed by such factors as: the age of the child; the child's individual capabilities, including intellectual and physical impairment; potential dangers; the foreseeability of injury; and past experience of loss. Generally speaking, staff owe children a duty to take reasonable care to protect them from foreseeable risk of injury. This manifests itself in many ways, including the duty: to supervise so that children comply with rules and practices designed for their own safety and that of others; to design and implement appropriate programmes and procedures to ensure the safety of children; to ensure that buildings, equipment, and so on are safe;

and to warn children about dangerous situations or practices (Criniti 2001).

It is in the performance of duty of care by teachers that personal and professional issues meet:

> *Teaching, this is a bit of an old-fashioned way of describing it, it is a service industry and, consequently, people who practise it have a sense of responsibility for their charges and their work. There are very few teachers who would allow difficult circumstances to upset their teaching too much. I am saying it is a belief about a responsibility. It is drummed into us that we are 'in loco parentis'. These kids are our kids. We are looking after these kids. Whether or not we accept that responsibility or see it, it IS [speaker's emphasis] there. It is part of the reason we will not let students out on the road at lunchtime, it is part of the reason we have rolls, why we have playground duty. It is the underlying factor as to why teachers do those jobs that they see as being part of the job of teaching. That is why schools have welfare programmes, because they realize they are looking after young people.*
>
> (Wendy, headteacher for 3 years)

Although the current political and educational climate can present a perspective contrary to this, one that is focused on the mechanics of teaching and learning with a concentration on academic outputs, the view expressed by Wendy is one held by teachers who see teaching as a vocation.

Teachers' roles

Teachers' professional roles involve informing students and having the answers. It is difficult, therefore, for teachers to put themselves in the role of not knowing what to say, a position frequently encountered in grief support. This is one predicament teachers experience in the roles they may be required to perform when addressing loss and grief issues. The other predicament encountered by teachers is the expression of emotion or the need to 'keep it together'. Each of these predicaments can be viewed as bi-polar 'either/or' positions. In practice, however, what occurs is often dependent on the teacher's perspective of the role they are playing – teaching subjects or teaching young people.

However, Leaman (1995) does not see it as a clash of professional roles. He suggests a different interpretation, believing that hiding one's feelings relates to promotional opportunities in the profession: 'Teachers who allow themselves to be upset by what they find in the classroom, or indeed outside of it, are not going to be highly respected by their colleagues, and are unlikely to be seen as prime candidates for promotion' (p. 62).

Some teachers are conscious of the varying roles they may be required to perform in a day, from being an information giver to lending a supportive ear:

*When I move into the senior classes, the subjects I teach are very academically oriented. I am trying with those kids to get them to score as many points as they can in their exams and assessments. So I have my academic hat on. When I move out of my **Faculty** area I have my welfare hat on. I am not so focused on what the children are achieving, but more concerned about them enjoying school and developing the socialization skills that schools hope to achieve. I change but there are some teachers who are narrower and are only interested in getting academic results.*

(Grant, welfare coordinator for 15 years)

Jeff, a deputy headteacher, recounted the judgement he made about the behaviour of a senior student whose attendance had fallen away after his father died. He, too, had experienced the death of a parent as an adolescent. His awareness of the impact of that on himself resulted in him dropping his role as a disciplinarian:

I think I was probably trying to offer him support. It is not so much 'you can lean on me' as 'you are not alone'. Just the knowledge that someone else has been there, that someone else has been through it, that it doesn't have to totally devour and consume you, eat you up and spit you out! It was a difficult situation. It is always difficult to deal with someone who is feeling that type of personal loss. You work with what you have got, with a sense of caring and I guess empathy. I have been there and it still hurts. I don't know that it helped him at all. But what else could I do? I could have divorced his circumstance and my past from the situation entirely and chastised him for being a naughty boy. But that didn't seem to be very productive. It was a case of trying to be helpful. That's the judgement you make. This exposes part of me that maybe I don't want exposed. In a situation like this you make a judgement about whether the kid can cope with it and the bias that I brought to it was a strong natural empathy for the situation.

(Jeff, deputy headteacher for 2 years)

Jeff's explanation indicates an insightful reflective ability about his role that enables him to develop awareness of his motives that he is able to clearly articulate and, therefore, justify his actions.

As well as disciplinary responsibilities, teachers have a standard educator role and a duty of care role. The latter can involve broad demands that include a supportive, pastoral care role as well as being an advocate in the school environment for children. Not only is there a breadth of responsibilities involved, but teachers interpret and practise these responsibilities in varying ways.

As an educator, teachers may encounter circumstances in the class-room that involve loss and grief. For example, many teachers were asked to explain a wide variety of issues after the in-depth media coverage of the planes hitting the World Trade Center in New York and people being seen jumping from windows. If a critical incident occurs in a school community, teachers may be called upon to convey the details to their class personally. That is, all teachers may be required to explain a death and to acknowledge grief reactions in the classroom with or without the aid of a support person. Ian relates how he told his grade four class about the sudden death of one of their classmates:

> *Then it was traumatic in actually trying to relay that information over to the children in the class. That was the very difficult part about it. The fact was that there was no means of communication with the parents at that time. So we did not have exact details. It was talking about Mark as a person and how he enjoyed his football, how he loved his football, how we would have to deal with the situation and just remembering Mark.*
>
> (Ian, deputy headteacher for 2 years)

Gail had been in her small semi-rural school for a long time, was known by many of the students and was perceived by other staff to have the desired personal qualities for telling students about death. She described her role:

> *I had a couple of instances where children had lost a parent. It just came naturally that I was the teacher who told the class, and talked to them about how they would respond to that student when they got back. It helped the class behave more naturally. I gave them some ideas what to say. I also talked with the student about what had been said to the class.*
>
> (Gail, teacher for 15 years)

It is important in these instances to respect the privacy of students. With older students it may be possible to negotiate what information and how the information will be given to the class. A complicating factor in **secondary schools** is that students attend many classes. Clusters of students, such as groupings of friends or sporting teams, may be a more desirable format. Teachers report the ongoing impact of an 'empty desk', when students leave the desk the dead student sat in unoccupied, so that there is a constant reminder to teachers and students alike. The issue of 'reminders' needs careful decision making as one primary school teacher explained:

> *The next day, they [the dead boy's classmates] wanted to put his photograph up on the display and that is what we did. We put the photograph up on the display board. We managed our way through the rest of that week. The*

children's work is kept in their own personal trays in a trolley within the classroom itself. I could not, for a whole term, literally touch that tray. I could not actually take David's label off that tray. The books that I took out of that tray and handed to the parents had gone, but the remaining things inside that tray, the pen and the pencil, still remained in that tray. I could not move it, it must have been for about two terms. Even when I did tear the label off, I could not throw it away, it was as though I was throwing the last pieces, the last remnants of his existence in the classroom, I could not do it. It was strange that the children kept saying, 'David's tray is still there!' And, of course, that was it. I had to just say, 'It is just staying there, just leave it!', I used to cut it off dead. I think they got over it quicker than I did, because they were saying to me, 'well get rid of the tray now', but I just could not do it.

(Ian, deputy headteacher for 2 years)

By his actions, Ian was conveying 'It is okay. David is still with us, if this happened to you, you would not be torn off and thrown out, you will stay here with us for a while'. He used this event to teach the students the value of life and the importance of remembering.

Students become upset in classrooms all the time and all teachers need to know how to respond to an upset child. Useful strategies for supporting a student include:

- avoiding directing attention or class focus towards the student;
- choosing a less public moment to ask if they are okay and giving them space within the classroom to be upset;
- offering them the chance to leave the room and get a drink or hand-kerchief and return when they are more composed;
- allowing them to go to a designated quiet place in the school or to the school nurse or a nominated person if they are available;
- offering a buddy to accompany them if immediate comfort is needed;
- following up with the student after the lesson; and
- setting a task for the other students while the teacher sits and talks with the upset student (Rowling 2000).

Some teachers are naturally inclined to a more pastoral or welfare attitude in their interactions with young people, whereas others take those roles as part of their position in a school. Teachers with these roles require a more in-depth knowledge about young people's grief reactions and the actions that the school needs to take. They need to be flexible in supporting a young person, having as their guiding philosophy the importance of hearing from the young people themselves. They need to find out what the young people are feeling and thinking, how they wish to be handled in the school in relation to their loss and the nature of the information to be disclosed and the form of its communication in the school. Harry, a year adviser, was supporting 13-year-old Allan whose parent had a terminal illness. Allan was happy for people in the school to know about the family's circumstances. Harry arrived at the action the school would take by talking with Allan and his parents. Harry related how this occurred after concern was expressed about Allan's misbehaviour at school:

I asked Allan's permission to talk to his teachers to give out some material. I said 'I wouldn't do anything unless I have your permission'. Allan was very pleased about that. He was quite happy [for me] to pass on the material to the teachers. I put the material together and wrote a letter saying 'This is confidential, Allan's mother is suffering from a terminal illness. This material may be helpful for you in understanding changes in behaviour. At the moment he is coping quite well, but you must expect that there will be changes in his behaviour as her condition deteriorates. If you want to talk any more about it come and see me'. I packaged it all up, put it in envelopes, sealed it and handed it to staff . . . I think it told him that I respected his privacy, that this was not an issue that I had ownership of, that it was his life we were dealing with here and that I didn't want to do anything that would cause him any difficulty. He seemed quite happy about that. I had an interesting response from one of the staff yesterday when I was giving out the material. They said, 'It comes as no surprise that he wants to be a kid at school'. I gleaned from that that there was a lack of maturity in behaviour. I said 'Well yes, he has to be an adult at home looking after his mother and sister, so you can certainly understand why he would want to be a kid at school'. His mother has about 6 months to live.

(Harry, year coordinator for 14 years)

Harry's report of his conversation conveys his respect for the student's privacy and demonstrates how the behaviour of students at school can be quite different from their behaviour at home. In conveying to other staff Allan's circumstances, Harry had been very careful to give Allan 'control' of the situation and attempt to ensure confidentiality. Teachers in roles like Harry's can clash with other staff when they act as an advocate for students. This is certainly the case when staff see leniency by colleagues as a weakness and they believe that the students 'should just pull themselves together'. Bill describes this clash:

As time went by we were caught in this situation where we had to be sympathetic to the kids, but also try not to sound like we were being door-mats for the students in the staff's eyes. We had to defend the kids in a way, but also be realistic. Asking ourselves 'Are they using this?' It was very hard to assess that.

(Bill, teacher for 9 years)

Such dilemmas are experienced continuously by those in support roles, especially when young people might be behaving in a manner judged by some staff not to be evidence of grieving, for example where senior boys play an intense game of basketball after the funeral of their peer. Most teachers would err on the side of leniency if the benefit to the group outweighs the need to curb the spurious behaviour of a few.

Staff in welfare roles also provide a link between the school and the family. This is an invaluable role for the school, as it signifies a school's recognition and commitment to continuity of care. In the case of a death in the family, students value teachers they perceive as being supportive, visiting the family at home and attending the funeral. It provides a sense of life going on for the student. Pre-planning needs to occur for home visits to families of different cultural backgrounds, as there may be customs and rituals that are unfamiliar to the teacher that need to be managed with sensitivity, for example decision making about a student's date of return to school. Smilansky (1987: 134) described such visits as 'a human act of caring, of sharing the child's pain, and it should be viewed as part of the professional responsibility of every member of staff'. Every member of staff may not feel comfortable with this role. It may also be inappropriate for staff who are concurrently experiencing grief in their personal lives to take on this professional responsibility.

A teacher may be required to take on the role of mediator, for example when there has been a critical incident and the media are waylaying students, pressurizing them to give comments. The media's presence can create secondary victims, for example students who see this as their 'moment of glory'. Dennis was aware of this possibility and advised students what to do:

> *I would talk with the students, going from class to class saying: 'now when you are dismissed today and you go outside, this is what you are going to encounter and this is what I suggest you do'. It was very difficult because of their maturity level and the point they were at in handling their grief. They wanted to talk about it. But the media was not the appropriate setting to talk about it. So they would get caught in a situation when they were going across the street to walk home or get onto a school bus. The reporter would get them talking about it, responding to questions and then they would get overcome with emotion, crying and upset. That is, of course, what the media wanted. The students just didn't have the maturity and skills necessary to handle it. What they needed to do was talk with counsellors in an appropriate setting rather than on the street.*
>
> (Dennis, deputy headteacher for 2 years)

Another mediating role involves establishing and maintaining links with outside service providers. Although many schools have access to services, some are remote from such services or the service has a limited number of staff. Staff in welfare roles need familiarity with outside agencies and the skills to refer students and families effectively. This is an area fraught with difficulty, as discussed in Chapter 9. Some of this difficulty arises from issues to do with confidentiality. Some schools have very clear systems for handling private and confidential student information, but no one teacher should be responsible for all these duties. A system of care is needed.

The school as a workplace

Although much of the focus of management of grief is on students, the school is also a workplace in which staff spend a significant amount of their time and where challenges related to grief and experiences of loss occur. In recent years, greater attention has been paid to the safety needs of staff, both from a legal point of view, under Occupational Health and Safety laws, and from the recognition of the impact of loss on teachers (Rowling 1995). The recognition of post-traumatic stress disorder in the workplace has also impacted on the provisions schools are making for their staff.

In a critical incident, attention often focuses on students, whereas the nature of the incident might mean that the needs of staff are paramount. A teacher recalls her experience:

That's the thing we found most lacking, the welfare and needs of staff were put on hold. Sometimes they do have to be put on hold while procedures are carried out. But sometimes it is not that way, sometimes the needs of staff are paramount and they have to be dealt with before the needs of students. It is up to the school team to identify that and put in the priorities.

(Sue, teacher for 15 years)

Unlike other organizations, schools have limited flexibility in their workplace practices. Teachers have to be in classrooms at specific times. They cannot start early and finish late or change their shifts, their time at work is prescribed. Teachers report coping with this limitation by using 'dosing' effectively – that is, switching off their personal lives when they enter the school gates, putting grieving on hold until they get home. So, is any flexibility possible for staff experiencing grief in their personal lives or who are affected by a critical incident in the school? One suggestion made by headteachers is a discretionary fund, with special relief made available from a central body to schools that have experienced a critical incident and where a number of staff have been affected. There are also (unofficial) school practices that can be modified for secondary staff. For example, the 'top drawer' approach is useful for those who have no lessons to teach in the morning or afternoon. They fill in a leave form, it is put in the headteacher's or deputy headteacher's top drawer and they go home or come in late the next morning. The form is torn up when the teacher arrives next on duty. In this way, the teacher and school are both covered in the event of some misadventure offsite, when the staff member is technically on duty.

One headteacher, Lucy, described her role as follows:

To let staff know I had empathy for what their experience is and to offer support in any way that I can. Maybe assist them with release time, which I have done before for teachers who have had parents who have died. We now have got personal leave as well as pressing domestic leave or a term like that. Often they will come and tell me if they are experiencing some problem within their personal life. We do have an access [employee assistance] programme that they can go to. I have to phone the office to tell them someone is going to use access and then they are not charged, or I put them in touch with a counselling service.

(Lucy, headteacher for 19 years)

Why should schools make provision for staff? There is evidence to suggest that grief diminishes energy, limits productivity and affects people's ability to think rationally. Motivation and creativity can also be affected (Lattanzi-Licht 2002). Because of their caring role for students, however, schools, unlike many other organizations, have the capacity to care for staff. They have knowledgeable staff who can provide technical information. Ideally, they have policies for or approaches to handling the private information of staff. However, the school supervisory staff may not get the information because the reactions of staff to personal and professional crises may be camouflaged: by beliefs about being strong and in control, or by medication, so they do not 'break down' in front of the students. At stake can be a teacher's feelings of competence and sense of direction. Teachers like others in society cope with loss in different ways, so their needs for support differ. Together with information, emotional support is frequently offered, but teachers in support roles also need confirmation that they are still being effective in their roles. Where conflict over management of events or students occurs, the moral support of colleagues is invaluable. These colleagues can be supportive by displaying ongoing interest in the welfare roles their peers may be struggling to perform. A useful strategy could be to acknowledge the stress and vulnerability of staff and, for a period of time, limit their exposure to students who present with emotionally charged problems.

Links into employee assistance programmes that are independent of the school may be useful. In the case of a loss of a family member, employees typically get three days bereavement leave. During this time, a great deal of support may be made available, but it is later, when others go back to their normal lives, that staff may need extra support and flexibility in the workplace. Sometimes this may happen informally with colleagues. A responsible and compassionate headteacher needs to have systems in place whereby those practices automatically come into operation. These will vary depending on the circumstances and the resources of the school. A compassionate approach will have long-term benefits for the school, such as a greater commitment from staff when they have experienced support that helps them integrate personal and work demands.

Sometimes the grief of teachers is not recognized. Gail recounted a story of the sudden death of a colleague in another school in a small semi-rural community:

> *The day the teacher from the other school in Neartown died, our critical incident plan fell down badly on the welfare of the teachers. The teacher had been a close personal friend and we were trying to hold ourselves together. It was the beginning of the day. We had been told to 'Go on class, you have to teach eight periods!' When it came to the day of the funeral, the headmaster didn't close the school. Half the staff went and half didn't. Many people were upset by that.*
>
> (Gail, teacher for 15 years)

In other instances, it may only be one staff member – often the class teacher – who is affected. They may feel alone and abnormal in their reaction if colleagues do not recognize their loss, as Ian recounts:

> *It was happening to me and it did not seem to be happening to everybody else. The world goes on around you, you are in your own little world. It is just like being in a goldfish bowl looking out, but it is not reality outside of you. This is the feeling that I got, that I was in a goldfish bowl, there was a big wide world going on outside and yet I could not get back into it, they could not get in to me, to understand me the way as I wanted them to understand me. They were acting just in a normal way and moving on. I think it would have been beneficial for me to know that there was some structure in place from the authority that was able to come in, support and advise and create the possibility of counselling for me as a person.*
>
> (Ian, deputy headteacher for 2 years)

Teachers bemoan the lack of support that schools receive from their systems. The devolution to local school management in many countries leaves schools without the resources and expert direction that was previously available.

Personal reactions

Teachers' personal reactions have already been alluded to in this chapter. Teachers who control their personal reactions in a critical incident may do so as a way of restoring balance if the normal school routine is disrupted. As already mentioned, other members of staff often remain ignorant of the private issues of a colleague. When the normal running of a school is disrupted, the hidden emotions of private grief may be aroused and, a teacher may exhibit an unexpectedly strong reaction, often triggered by the resurgence of feelings alluded to in Chapter 11. Janice reported the reaction of one of her staff at the first anniversary service for a student who had died in an accident in view of other students:

> *In the morning the students did a small memorial service in the theatre at 8.00 am, before school started and we all went. The girls did it. They sang their songs again. It was very well done. The thing that finished them off was a member of staff who wasn't actually the dead girl's form tutor but was very involved with them. She went up and read her ideas about death, very emotionally. None of them realized the impact which the death of the student had had on other people. But it wasn't the impact of the student's death on the teacher, she was grieving for her mother, who had died. The teacher had coped well at the time, but it came out at this service. I found that amazing! I knew why the teacher was upset, the girls certainly didn't. But they were shocked that a member of staff should act like that because we had all been so professional, of course she had feelings and that came out.*
>
> (Janice, headteacher for 16 years)

Teachers do become connected to their students. Guy had been teaching for many years at a school where two students were killed in a horrendous accident at a school activity. He had taught the students for the first two years of their secondary school:

> *You see them every day for most of the year, you watch them grow, so there's obviously, there's kind of bonds develop. So that brings you fairly close. When you confront these big issues, like their deaths, the fact that they are young kids, it really spins you around and next time you want to be prepared for that. It's very painful for yourself, plus you want to, as a teacher, be there for the kids.*
>
> (Guy, teacher for 9 years)

This personal engagement and commitment to the well-being of students involves risk for a teacher as the boundaries between the professional and the personal become blurred. This is a particular risk for those with a year adviser or pastoral care role. If something traumatic happens in their school community, they are likely to be affected in several ways. First, they are affected because of their sense of responsibility for students and perhaps their perception of failure in their role. Second, they may be affected as a result of beliefs about their role, beliefs about controlling or repressing emotions, 'being strong' when their natural inclination is the reverse. Third, they can be affected if they are called upon to provide support when, unlike emergency workers called in at times of critical incidents, teachers will have personal connections with the people affected. The suppression of their own feelings to support the students and the lack of recognition of their need for support by school leaders can place them at personal risk.

Harry explained his predicament in this way:

> I don't know how to disengage. I've been reading a play with year 11, 'Whose life is it anyway?' One of the things that the main character is concerned about is the way professionals objectify themselves. I think the point there is that he wants people to interact with him as a human being and it is the wardsman who does this. I think in this counselling role that I am engaged in, I think it is hard for me to disengage, because to be fully honest and open with Gary it has to take part of your person. You are giving part of yourself to that person. To be professional about it is to cut that off. I don't know how to do that and I wonder whether that is such a good idea?
>
> (Harry, year coordinator for 5 years)

Conclusion

Teachers need support and guidance to maintain clearly defined professional boundaries so that vulnerable students do not read more into the relationship. There are other risks for teachers untrained and unsupported in their pastoral roles. Teachers' interactions with children may trigger 'the child in the teacher' – that is, connect with their childhood losses. Also, teachers may be unaware of the need to guard against using the classroom or their one-to-one work with students as a way of working through their own grief, although being able to talk openly about one's loss can be healing and a good role model. Teachers may also fail to recognize the limitations of their role, for despite their best intentions they may not be able to do much to improve some children's lives. Teachers and headteachers who appoint staff to student support roles need to consider carefully staff members' readiness, both emotionally and content wise, to work with students in this area and take responsibility for monitoring the impact on the teacher of their pastoral care work.

Implications for practice

- It is important for teachers to familiarize themselves with strategies that can support an upset student, such as those outlined on page 37.
- Staff in welfare roles require access to professional development opportunities relating to grief and loss and mental health promotion. This will help to ensure they have the depth of understanding and skills necessary to support students experiencing loss and grief.
- Establishing a 'system of care' within the school will demonstrate the school's commitment to the welfare of students. Within this system of care, forming links with families and external agencies is essential.
- Critical incidents often attract media attention. Teachers must be well briefed on how to handle the media themselves and how to advise students on what to do if approached by the media.
- A critical incident provides an opportunity to teach students about loss and grief.
- Teachers may suppress their feelings during a critical incident, believing they need to maintain composure for the sake of the students. This can place some students at risk. Support structures for staff must also be developed and implemented. This could involve access to services independent of the school.

Further reading

Egan, G. (1994) *The Skilled Helper*, 5th edn. Pacific Grove, CA: Brooks/Cole.

Lattanzi-Licht, M. (2002) Grief and the workplace: positive approaches, in K.J. Doka (ed.) *Disenfranchised Grief: New Directions, Challenges, and Strategies for Practice*. Champaign, IL: Research Press.

Leaman, O. (1995) *Death and Loss: Compassionate Approaches in the Classroom*. London: Cassell.

CHAPTER 4

Grief and the classroom

Introduction

The losses that young people can experience, with their accompanying emotional and behavioural responses, are diverse: the loss of health through illness or accident; the loss of expectation, such as failing to make a team; the death of a beloved pet; and the loss of self-esteem through a friend's rejection or a failure in school. As detailed in Chapter 2, grief reactions are responses to these losses. Although the diversity of loss that young people experience through psychosocial transitions was delineated over a decade ago (Parkes 1988), there has not been a concomitant shift in education about the impact of these events. Death education has been the main thrust of curriculum approaches in the United States from the early 1980s (Eddy and Alles 1983). The basic orientation of these approaches was in exploring affective responses and a cognitive understanding of death, an approach that has provoked criticism (Weekes and Johnson 1992).

In England, texts have looked at loss in general (Ward and Houghton 1988; Plant and Stoate 1989; Leaman 1995), but there is still a tendency for an overtone of a crisis intervention mode and a focus on expression of emotions. In *Loss and Change*, Plant and Stoate (1989) showed a concern for exploring emotional responses and developing an understanding of grief. They also suggested that some of the activities could be used in a 'crisis response', when an individual child is bereaved or when the class or school as a whole are responding to a 'community' grief. Rowling and Holland (2000) confirmed this intervention orientation of the curriculum, compared with a prevention and skills for life approach in Australia. Twenty-nine per cent of respondent schools in Australia included grief education as part of the ongoing curriculum and not as an *ad hoc* topic (Rowling and Holland 2000). In contrast, only 9 per cent of schools in England included grief as part of the ongoing curriculum. This latter finding could be explained by the prescriptive nature of the National Curriculum and, therefore, the limited opportunity for the inclusion of education about grief and pressure to achieve standards. More recently, Australian Government funded resource materials on loss and grief as part of a mental health promotion project have been produced and disseminated nationally (Rowling 2000).

Teaching about loss and grief continues to be controversial and sensitive. For many education and health professionals, it is still viewed solely as an intervention to help solve a problem or prevent the development of problems. Discussing death after the experience in a school community is probably the most difficult time to tackle this emotionally charged issue. A crisis-orientated approach is not an approach that acknowledges the 'normality of grief'. Zisook (1987: 11) described the aims of classroom lessons as 'normalization through education', a process that can help grieving young people to realize that their experiences are a normal part of the grieving process. The school environment, through its curriculum, structures and processes, can contribute to this normalization. A crisis approach also does not acknowledge the school as a community, as a social system, which has the capacity to provide support (Petersen and Straub 1992) and to provide opportunities for young people to test new behaviours, develop conceptual understandings and share different and similar ideas about loss and grief.

As identified in Chapter 1, the sensitivity of loss and grief arises from the political, social and cultural contexts that impact on the issue. Key elements for teachers and students are the emotionality and meaning that are involved in loss and grief in the classroom context. Students' personal reactions and experiences of loss also impact on classroom discussion and activity. These are delineated in other chapters. Controversy about inclusion of loss and grief in the curriculum echoes themes already identified, such as privacy and belief in reliance on personal resources, a debate about usurping the role of the family and the aims of schooling.

Quality teaching and effective learning about loss and grief draw on social learning theory and life skills training. An underpinning premise is that learners are active participants in their learning.

Theoretical perspectives

There are many aspects of learning that have shaped the teaching of sensitive issues. Particular attention is paid here to social learning theory and life skills education.

Social learning theory

This theory, which was originally developed by Bandura (1986), has been influential in several fields, including education and health promotion. Two elements of this theory that are important for this chapter relate to observational learning: role modelling, or learning by practising behaviour observed in others; and vicarious experience, reflecting on and analysing experience that is observed.

Life skills education

The World Health Organization (WHO) suggested that life skills education should be composed of the following:

- Life skills, defined as 'abilities for adaptive and positive behaviour, that enable individuals to deal effectively with the demands and challenges of everyday life' (WHO 1993: 3). These skills are the abilities to promote mental health and competence in young people as they face the realities of life.
- A child-centred and activity orientated methodology.
- A philosophical belief in the need to provide the opportunity for young people to take action (Birrell Wiesen and Orley 1996).

Life skills education can be effectively developed through curricula in schools. The pedagogy involves cooperative learning, participative activities and experiential learning. Life skills, such as critical thinking, self-awareness, coping with emotions and empathy, are taught within the context of health and social issues. Although the role of the environment is acknowledged, the main focus is the individual (Birrell Wiesen and Orley 1996).

Teaching about loss and grief

Many teaching resources are available that contain suggested lessons or activities for groups about loss and grief (Ward and Houghton 1988; O'Toole 1991; Rowling 2000). These are not the focus here, however. Rather, this chapter concentrates on theoretical and practical issues involved in curriculum implementation, exploring the controversies that exist and the challenges teachers experience. Areas to be explored include the content and process of curriculum implementation and the views and experiences of teachers and students. Criteria for choosing resource materials are provided at the end of the chapter. Unlike other parts of the curriculum, teaching about loss and grief requires 'readiness to teach' both emotionally and in terms of content. A direct factual approach designed not to frighten needs to be adopted. To ensure a balanced approach in deciding on content and process, the value in pursuing particular issues and choosing resource materials, a teacher may need to reflect: 'Have I achieved a balance between focusing on information about grief experiences and the emotional responses of students?'

Content

An ongoing controversy is what should be taught to young people about loss and grief. This is not a simple question. It involves not only the skills of the educator and the learning environment (to be discussed later in this chapter), but also the learning context of the sessions, either a narrow focus on death or a broader focus on loss and change experiences. There are several formats for educational sessions, ranging from sequential lessons in a mandated area of the curriculum such as health education to a 'special event' from a bereavement expert in response to a critical incident in a school. Concerns that 'lessons' about mental health, loss and grief or suicide create anxiety often arise when the learning context is not clearly established (Schmitt and Ellman 1991). Additionally, researchers often use measures of anxiety immediately after a lesson to assess impact (Shaffer *et al.* 1990). Raising anxiety will be discussed later in this chapter, but it is natural that a lesson about loss and grief or a 'special event' by an outside educator would create anxiety in young people who may be encountering these sensitive issues for the first time.

Education about loss and grief may occur in a variety of contexts. These are linked to the aims of schooling, academic or pastoral (Willcock 1996). If the aims are of a prevention–intervention orientation, they are more likely to be linked to pastoral care, with the learning context being of an extracurricula nature. If they have an academic purpose, with an educational aim of 'the value of life and the importance of quality relationships' (Willcock 1996: 106), then they are likely to be accepted as part of the curriculum, such as health education or life skills. Although 'academic' may be interpreted solely in terms of the traditional curriculum areas of maths, English and science, for young people to be equipped in the twenty-first century, they require cognitive, affective and behavioural learning about health and social issues. In this sense, 'academic' is not meant to convey a prescriptive, inflexible structure, but rather the existence of a legitimate area of scholarship, school health education. As a senior student commented:

> *It's not going to do you any good if you've got a wonderful mark in maths if your personal life is totally ruined, because you did not deal with a problem properly. It's balance, a well rounded education.*
>
> (Nicole, 16-year-old student)

This student valued learning in the affective area. She was one of the senior students who had access to a mandated 25 hours on health and social issues in their last two years of secondary school. The broader learning context was personal development and health education, a sequential area of study from primary school through to grade 10 in secondary school (New South Wales Board of Studies 1991). That is, there was a learning context in the school structure for loss and grief curriculum, although in the senior years it was not a compulsory area of study.

The focus on death education or bereavement education was charac-teristic of much of the work with and in schools during the 1980s. This led to the adoption of specific learning contexts that still exist:

- Teachers with an interest in teaching about loss and grief use and modify existing materials, such as storybooks for young children and various stimulus materials for adolescents. These teachers may or may not have had training. This will be discussed in a later chapter, but a lack of training has important implications for the outcomes for both the teacher and the students.
- A special 'unit' may be implemented as part of pastoral care or tutor group activities, again with or without training for the teacher.
- The special 'unit' might be conducted by a bereavement specialist from an outside agency. This person will be trained in bereavement but may have limited knowledge of the students and will not be available to the students once issues have been raised in the sessions.
- Teachable moments that arise as a result of school community losses or world events with widespread media coverage can also be the learning context.

The way the school includes learning about loss and grief will indicate its importance in the minds of many school community members. The more the learning is part of the ongoing structure of the school, the more value it will be seen to have.

The position adopted in this book is that the broader perspective of loss and grief, rather than a sole focus on just death or bereavement, is more appropriate for the school curriculum. An underlying premise in decision making about topics is the importance of engaging students. In focusing on loss, there is a much greater chance of linking with students' experi-ences because of the universality of these grief encounters. A focus on loss provides depth and breadth of the cognitive (information for young people), affective (emotional responses) and behavioural (reactions taken and actions to take).

There are two things that need to be considered when deciding on which topics to include. First, the developmental age of the students. As identified in Chapter 2, the cognitive and emotional development of students affect the choice of topics and learning experiences. A sequential curriculum revisits issues as students mature. For young children, their limited ability to think abstractly is an important consideration. Although facts are important, technical details about the biological aspects of death will need to be limited. Additionally, being protective of children and focusing solely on death can result in teachers limiting discussions to the deaths of animals and not including human beings. Using 'loss' as a starting point will allow issues to arise from the students' experiences, thereby achieving a better match with students' development. A key message for young children who may be very fearful, is that adults are present to protect them at home and at school.

A 13-year-old boy reported that he kept it to himself that his father had died because he had observed another boy being teased about not having a father, something that had made him cry. Grant explained the boy's behaviour in this way:

> *They are very conscious of reactions of other people on something that is personal to them. Boys in particular don't like to be seen crying at that age. Maybe they don't want to be seen as different – you've got a parent alive, I don't have a parent alive. Maybe they haven't had any form of education about grief. Maybe they've been encouraged to bottle up their grief and not show their grief or express their grief to others. Maybe it's a feeling of shame.*
> (Grant, teacher for 15 years)

The second thing that needs to be considered is the skills content. The basic orientation of early approaches to death education was in exploring affective responses and a cognitive understanding of death, dying and stages of grief. In the last decade, there has been a broadening of topics to include separation and divorce and other loss experiences. Together with this broadening has been the recognition of the need to focus on skills such as help seeking and help receiving (Rowling 2000).

Although the capacity to be flexible in teaching about loss and grief is important, there are essential 'content' messages that should frame the curriculum:

- People react differently to loss experiences, so each personal experience is unique.
- There are strategies to help people cope with their own or a friend's loss experiences.
- Everybody needs to be able to identify sources of help.
- People from different cultural, ethnic and religious backgrounds may cope with loss in different ways (Rowling 2000).

Suicide as a topic in the curriculum is discussed in Chapter 10.

Process

The 'how' of loss and grief education includes the learning environment and the teaching strategies that create opportunities for students to be active participants. A senior student recounts her experience of this:

> She [the teacher] was sort of nice and calm and she got us to talk about how WE [student's emphasis] felt, not just this is how PEOPLE [student's emphasis] feel.
>
> (Beth,16-year-old student)

This strategy of drawing on students' experiences was emphasized by a parent, who was potentially supportive of teaching about loss and grief, depending on the way teachers did it:

> They need to find out from the students, their experiences.
>
> (Mrs Papadopolous, a parent)

Another student said:

> This is the first time we discussed about death, but everyone was open. It is the kind of lesson where everyone can share their feelings.
>
> (Nina, 16-year-old student)

The learning environment needs to involve trust, rapport and respect between students and between the teacher and the students. Within this classroom environment, issues of privacy, those who are talking and those who are talked about need to be addressed. Class rules may need to be established about this and, where necessary, reminders may be given at the beginning of lessons during which disclosure of personal thoughts and feelings might occur. These rules might include agreement not to name people who are being talked about. Students might also need guidance about appropriate behaviour in the lessons. Additionally, a teacher might need to use 'protective interrupting' – that is, a gentle caution if a student begins adding personal details that they might later regret. A teacher may suggest the student substitutes phrases such as 'I know someone who . . .' and 'What if a parent said . . .' In this context, a teacher needs to avoid any hint that what students have said is of no importance and be respectful of experiences and feelings students wish to share. Private reflection can be encouraged and respected.

There are three generic skills that all teachers, but particularly those involved in loss and grief education, need:

- a wide variety of teaching approaches to match the learning styles of students;

- a flexible approach to curriculum planning and implementation to adapt to students' interests and experiences; and
- a reflective stance to their teaching practice so that they can take action to improve teaching performance.

For the students, communication skills are essential life skills at all ages and can be strengthened by loss and grief education. The skills to be learned are being able and prepared, to listen to others, to express feelings in a variety of ways, to provide help and support and to seek help when necessary. All these need to be addressed and practised.

Techniques for loss and grief education

Many teachers make effective use of the arts in teaching about loss. Storybooks provide an opportunity for learning through vicarious experience either through silent reading or as a stimulus to a class discussion. Use of literature as a means of helping young people relies on an emotional engagement of the reader and the literature read. Books must be realistic in the coverage of the issues for the developmental age of the audience. They should also present correct facts about the issues and hope, but not a false sense of hope. Depending on the children's developmental age, areas can be highlighted where there are differences of opinion about issues (Pardeck 1994). Silverman (2000: 242) warns of the need for careful choice. Materials should include rituals associated with death, 'not talk about recovery or getting over it, but should allow children to find ways to remember and to keep a connection with the deceased'. This last point reflects a shift in understanding from 'getting over' to 'continuing bonds' (Klass *et al.* 1996), where young people find a place in their memories for who or what has been lost.

Literature, across the broad spectrum of prose and poetry reading, writing, participating in drama activities and watching performances, helps in expression and experiences of grief. All these forms provide for learning by imitation, as well as opportunities to test out new behaviours. Music can be particularly valuable with adolescents, because it is such an important part of their lives. Not only do the lyrics express the concerns and experiences of young people, they also serve to give them space and validation (Skewes 1999). When in crisis, young people are drawn to songs because they are perceived as offering them true understanding. Adolescents who choose private means of grieving may be locking themselves in their rooms and turning up the music (Skewes 1999). While in music therapy the therapeutic relationship is addressed alongside the music, in a classroom environment it might be more appropriate for the teacher to model the sharing of songs that have meaning and inviting students to do the same. Song sharing can be valuable if students are involved in planning a memorial service for a peer. Analysis and discussion of lyrics in songs could also increase young people's understanding of grief.

The purpose of these techniques – to provide stimulus for dialogue and expression of feelings – has to be kept in mind. Caution needs to be exercised in their use, noting that in a classroom environment they are not for clinical interpretation.

Stimulus materials can provide opportunities for vicarious learning. I observed a lesson about grief with senior students that was conducted about eight weeks before a car accident that involved some of them. The teacher had forewarned the class of the topic. I had also observed several previous lessons, so the group were relaxed about my presence. The teacher introduced the lesson by distributing a bulletin from her son's school about the death of one of the school's year 11 students in a bus accident, a death witnessed by the bus load of students. The class was hushed as they read it to themselves. Later in a small group discussion with the author (Louise), students (pseudonyms) described their responses:

Louise:	*It was hard to believe that, given that situation, that is what could happen.*
Natasha:	*Not just that, but three-quarters of this school catch buses home. Something could happen just like that! Anybody at this school. No warning. No-one tells you, tomorrow your friend is going to die in a bus accident. It brings up a lot of issues.*
Franco, Leila, Nina:	*Yeah.*
Otto:	*Knock on wood* [knocking on the table].

Relationship between teacher and students

It is not just the choice of teaching and learning strategies that is important, but the nature of teacher–student interactions in these lessons. One characteristic of these interactions is the use by teachers of their personal experience. Their day-to-day work is about finding ways to help young people understand academic topics by using examples and connecting with similar concepts. In teaching about topics that have moral and legal implications, such as drug abuse and sexuality, teachers usually avoid the use of personal experience. However, research on loss and grief has identified the consistent use of personal anecdotes (Rowling 1996b). This personal disclosure involves risk, the teachers leaving themselves open to ridicule by students and risking their professional image. But they do it because they feel a personal connection between themselves and their students is important. Grant spoke as follows to his students:

> I said to them: 'At times during this session, I will talk about things that have happened in my life; if you want to ask questions about them, let me finish and then ask them'. That's what I said to the kids. I also said there will be times when I need to talk about that to help you people. If you think I'm forcing something on you let me know please, and stop me.
>
> (Grant, teacher for 15 years)

Not only do teachers use the recounting of personal experiences to engage the students in a vicarious learning process, but also to provide a role model. Grant told the students about the sudden death of his best friend's wife and about crying at the funeral. Although the students were quiet, Grant believed they were still involved. I asked what he thought was going through their heads. He replied:

> This person's real . . . [pause] . . . Maybe it is okay to cry, maybe there IS [Grant's emphasis] nothing wrong with crying. Here's a person, this is a self-perception of me in this school, here is a person who is seen to be friendly to every child in the school, spilling out a personal experience of himself, telling US [Grant's emphasis] he has actually cried, when we have never seen him cry. But telling us of a time when he has. Those sorts of things I think probably went through their heads. I think they were, not happy, happy is the wrong word, they had that sense of – feeling fine in themselves because this man spoke about something that was really an important event in his life.
>
> (Grant, teacher for 15 years)

Grant recognized the quiet in the classroom as silent processing. During a follow-up interview, I pressed Grant to explain to me what he meant by 'feeling fine in themselves because this man spoke about something that was really an important event in his life'. His response was an exposition of his philosophy of teaching about loss and grief – that is, using personal experience – and what he sees as the purposes of that teaching, notably to open up values debates for students:

> Because I want the kids in this school to know that here is a man who can talk about himself, about his feelings and I want to be the person who can use himself as an example.
>
> (Grant, teacher for 15 years)

Respect was a characteristic of these interactions: that of the teacher for the student in trusting the students' handling of the personal information; and that of the student for the teacher in that students saw the teacher's disclosure as evidence of their 'being human'. Personal connections with teachers were very important in that they helped to make students feel like individuals rather than just one of many people in a school. The self-disclosure by teachers was seen as natural behaviour, of being a 'human being', as this interchange exemplifies:

Tessa: *She told us about her brother and that, I was really surprised with that, because I didn't know – the teacher telling us something like that. [The teacher's brother had died at age 19]. Sort of shocked me at first, but then I thought 'Oh yeah! She is just trying to be like one of us'. I thought it was really good.*
Louise: *Was she trying to be like you?*
Beth: *Becoming human probably.*
Louise: *Is that unusual for teachers?*
Simon: *Yes.*
Beth: *Not Mrs Bailey, she is like that all the time. It is being aware of us. A lot of teachers are not in tune with the kids.*

(Group Interview, year 11)

These are the experiences and actions of Australian teachers. Using personal experience has been found to be more common in Australia than in England (Rowling and Holland 2000). The use of personal anecdotes could conflict with existing recommendations in the literature on grief counselling. Those in a supporting or counselling role are cautioned about the use of their own experience, so that it is not interpreted as a prescriptive way to grieve and that they are not using the situation to work through their own grief (Worden 1991). But schools are a different environment from that normally encountered during counselling. Relationships already exist between students and teachers. In schools, young people look continually to adults for models of behaviour. In sharing their experiences, teachers model open and honest ways of behaving as well as attitudes accepting of the right to cry and to express or talk about feelings. But good practice dictates that teachers need to be careful not to suggest that their behaviour should be a model for the students. Rather, they should use their experience as a springboard for the students' own discussions.

It also requires a shift in role in the classroom from being a teacher, a giver of facts, to a facilitator, an aid in the learning process. This can be a difficult shift, from having the answers or directing behaviour to respecting others' values and engaging in dialogue. One teacher described the qualities needed in this way:

It is not knowledge teachers are very keen to impart knowledge. It is discussing issues in an effective way and relating to students in a special way. They basically respect kids and that the kids relate to them in a positive and open way, even though the teachers may have vastly different values than what the students do. They are not judgemental about the values that the students hold, so that there is room for movement and agreement to discuss issues that don't threaten them. Adopt the stance that from an educational point of view we don't all have to agree.

(Gail, teacher for 14 years)

It can threaten a teacher's comfort level, as discussions may go off on a tangent and there is the ever present pressure to get through the prescribed content. Although Pam had been a teacher for 16 years, she had never taught about grief before:

I've never done anything on grief. At first I felt a little doubtful. The students tended to go on to different things and they brought up cultural things [about death] themselves, which was good. I tended to go with what they wanted to speak about. I didn't get deeply involved in their experiences either. I didn't want it to be a big delving session. I didn't know whether you need to or not. I let them say as much as they wanted to say. It was amazing how many of them have had experiences. Horrific things . . . fishing a head out of a river and a teacher actually had a heart attack while he was teaching them. He didn't actually die in front of them. He was taken to hospital and then died. One boy was talking about his parents separating. He was the only one who identified that as a loss, whereas others were thinking of grandma dying. But I just let them go. I didn't get deep. I sort of touched on a few different things and didn't say – 'Now how did you feel?' I didn't carry it on too much. I said, 'Anyone who wants to tell us'. The ones that wanted to speak did and the ones that didn't . . . but they were all involved. They were good listeners, but that worked well.

(Pam, tezacher for 11 years)

Training for increasing skills and levels of comfort is discussed in more detail in Chapter 12.

The impact of loss and grief education

One consistent concern expressed about including loss and grief in the curriculum is that it will create anxiety in students. As already described, the learning environment and the teaching process are vital elements in loss and grief education. After observing a lesson taught to senior students, I had a discussion with a group of them. Although the students valued the lesson, they didn't necessarily enjoy it. They experienced fear and anxiety about what could happen in the future. But they still thought it should be discussed. They made comments such as:

It turned out good [sic]. It turned up things I didn't know; I found it interesting to talk about feelings that you had; You have to talk about it, be aware of it. It is not something you can take easily; It gives you ideas about how to explain yourself if you were in that situation, to watch what they are doing.

For a primary school class, who spend most of their time with the one teacher, trust and safety in that environment as well as the teacher's knowledge of her or his students helps to limit the anxiety.

The senior students also appreciated learning in the school environment about how other people, particularly their peers, have adapted. They reported it gave them models of ways of behaving:

I was pleased we talked about a variety of topics, especially death, as it helped me understand about death and how we can cope with our grief and others' grief.

I was surprised to see how easy it was to talk about things that hurt.

I was surprised that someone else had the same problem as me and made me feel 'normal'.

I was surprised that we did talk about death but it was a good topic, although it isn't a nice thought though.

This last comment highlights the ambivalence experienced by these students. Simon, a 16-year-old, made a distinction between talking about loss in the school environment and the family – *'They [his parents] always try to tell me how to feel and I don't like that!'* – and the discussion in the group – *'People in the group were not trying to tell me how to feel, they were saying, "There are variations in how you feel and it is okay to feel like that"'.* Students like Simon valued the openness in discussions with teachers and recognized that they were different from discussions he might have with his parents.

Quality loss and grief education

Willcock (1996), an English journalist who went to America to investigate death education – 'another wacky aberration from abroad' (p. 101) – concludes his account as follows:

If death education can be true to its role and be led by the needs of the students rather than the whims of educators or the voices of critics, it will provide an important resource needed to meet the emotional crises that threatens today's youth.

(Willcock 1996: 109)

In classroom interactions, the teacher is not a social worker, but an educator who guides and facilitates to help young people acquire skills to adapt to current and future losses.

Quality practice, with all sensitive issues covered in the curriculum, requires that parents are informed of the school's programme, in this case loss and grief, and invited to discuss content with teaching staff. This gives staff an extra opportunity to learn about events in young people's lives that may impact on their reactions to lessons, both positively and negatively. It may also be valuable for a class teacher to forewarn students about lesson content and establish protective procedures for them such as 'It's okay to cry', 'If you are upset, you can leave the room', 'You don't have to talk, you can sit and listen'. These guidelines need to be established within existing school rules regarding 'what happens to students out of the classroom during lesson times'. Determining procedures beforehand with other staff such as the school nurse, school psychologist and pastoral care co-ordinator as to action for upset students is part of the responsible behaviour for teaching about loss and grief.

There are many storybooks, resource materials and agencies that are available to assist in education about loss and grief. Teachers need to exercise care in their selection of these. Guidelines for this choice include that the material or presentation:

- is appropriate for the target audience and takes into account the potential impact on young people and teachers;
- recognizes the complexity of grief and people's reactions;
- uses visual material only to link in with the written text or presentation, not to provide shock value;
- aims to increase young people's understanding of loss and grief and develop skills to adapt;
- includes sections on help seeking and help receiving;
- uses an instructional mode that suits the target audience and is participant-centred;
- respects the diversity of experiences, beliefs and attitudes of the group.

Conclusion

Effective teaching about loss and grief involves acknowledgment of the breadth of loss experiences and responses of young people, accounts for their developmental age, includes adequate attention to skill development and involves parents. It occurs in a learning environment characterized by trust, rapport and mutual respect and aims to make a contribution to positive mental health outcomes for young people.

Children and adolescents have, or will, experience some form of loss in their lives. Although teaching about loss and grief is controversial and sensitive, it can help normalize grief and assist young people to recognize that their experiences are a natural part of the grieving process.

Implications for practice

- Teaching about loss and grief must include strategies that actively involve students in their learning.
- Focus on loss and grief rather than on 'death'. This will maximize the opportunity to engage students actively by linking their experiences of loss to the curriculum.
- When designing loss and grief curriculum, ensure the essential 'content messages' outlined on page 51 are used as a framework for this.
- Establish class rules regarding privacy and confidentiality.
- Providing personal anecdotes can help develop rapport with students and can also provide them with a model of behaviour.
- Consult with welfare staff within the school to have procedures in place if students get upset.
- Students, particularly older ones, believe it is important to discuss loss and grief.
- Parents need to be informed about the school's programme and provided with the opportunity to discuss this with staff.
- Use the guidelines on page 59 to help make decisions about resource materials and agencies to assist in education about loss and grief.

Further reading

Leaman, O. (1995) *Death and Loss: Compassionate Approaches in the Classroom.* London: Cassell.

Rowling, L. (2000) *MindMatters: A Whole School Approach to Loss and Grief.* Canberra: Mental Health Promotion Branch, Commonwealth Department of Health and Aged Care (available at http://www.curriculum.edu.au/mindmatters).

Rowling, L. and Holland, J. (2000) Grief and school communities: the impact of social context, a comparison between Australia and England, *Death Studies,* 24(1): 15–24.

Ward, B. and Houghton, P. (1988) *Good Grief: Talking and Learning about Loss and Death.* London: Jessica Kingsley.

CHAPTER 5

Critical incident management

We developed a policy to deal with critical incidents, because we were aware they are going to happen, that the world is not easily controlled and there are going to be incidents that happen and cut across your bow all the time. They are going to unsettle your peace.

(Matt, headteacher for 10 years)

Introduction

The management of critical incidents exemplifies global changes in the demands on, and expectations of, schools in their duty of care for students and staff. Modern communication systems mean that for young people the 'innocence' about death and violence can no longer be maintained. Protection by 'non exposure' has been diminished; parents and school personnel are no longer able to 'insulate' those in their care. This global communication network results in immediacy and detailed display of war. The hurtling between buildings of scud missiles in cities in Iraq in the Gulf War was watched by the children of service personnel serving in that conflict. The explicit visual and auditory access that the coverage conveyed brought reality to the children of the conflict in which their parents were participating. Similarly, the image of the hijacked plane hitting the World Trade Center in New York on 11 September 2001 was re-played from every angle to television viewers around the world. It is, therefore, understandable that children in schools in Sydney under international flight paths wrote stories and drew pictures of planes crashing into their school.

These events also affect adults in care-giving roles. Horrific events shake core beliefs about the way of the world. Cognitive dissonance

– reality clashing with beliefs – is experienced by adults, leaving them uncertain, struggling to understand something that is incomprehensible. This struggle is all the more poignant for care-givers such as teachers who grapple to find explanations to the questions children in their care ask. These are children who look to teachers for 'the answers'.

As indicated in Chapter 1, critical incidents now have a higher profile in schools because of schools' fears of public scrutiny and the increased awareness of the impact of these events on school communities. This has resulted in a major shift in thinking, from perceiving critical incidents as events experienced by individuals who need support and understanding to events that impact on the school as an organization. Key themes throughout this chapter include safety and control as restorative mechanisms.

What is a critical incident?

A critical incident is defined as a situation faced by members of the school community that causes them to experience unusually strong emotional reactions that have the potential to interfere with their ability to function either at the time the incident occurs or later (Sheehan *et al.* 2000: 31). The deaths of students or staff members, particularly when they are on the school premises or involved in extra curricular activities, are easily recognizable as critical incidents. There are, however, cumulative happenings or factors that can magnify subsequent events, thereby intensifying emotional responses in the hours, days and weeks afterwards, and re-casting happenings as critical incidents. The factors that can 'create' critical incidents and also impact on the outcome of any critical incident are:

- the presence or absence of a school-developed critical incident management plan;
- the critical incident management model in operation and the availability of outside help suited to the incident;
- insufficient information available to school community members;
- intensive or adverse media coverage; and
- the nature of the events.

The presence or absence of a school-developed critical incident management plan

'In life there are occasional moments that remain with you forever . . . 21 October 1988 will always be that sort of day and that sort of memory, because tragedy struck Streetly School, where I was headteacher at the time' (Shears 1995: 241). These are the words of John Shears as he details the experience of his school community and the impact on himself of the death of a student and a teacher, who were members of a school party of 23, when the cruise ship *SS Jupiter* was sunk in the Mediterranean. He recommends: 'the main lesson to learn is that of being prepared' (Shears 1995: 253).

School personnel sometimes believe that as critical incidents differ, there is little value in having a school-developed management plan. Key elements, however, occur in all incidents. These can be accounted for in a generic plan that is proactive and based on good risk management principles. Critical incidents impact on individuals who need support, but they are also collective experiences in schools that require a management and organizational response. They are events that affect a number of people and the functioning of an organization. They produce a complexity of responsibilities and require a staged process of management. In the implementation of a plan, the involvement of some people or steps may be eliminated because of the nature of the incident. Without a plan, however, school personnel can be so enmeshed in the circumstances of the event that they overlook vital support elements. There is an important difference between an emergency evacuation plan such as for fire drills and a critical incident management plan. The former focuses on mechanical and technical issues, whereas the latter includes these together with a plan for the management of personnel and their possible responses.

A plan provides for allocation of specific role responsibilities among members of staff. They should be roles for which staff have been prepared beforehand. It does not rely on the presence of the headteacher in the school to direct action. Rather, the management of an incident is achieved through identification of the roles to be performed, the roles being allocated according to people's strengths not their position in the school hierarchy. This structure gives authority to people who, in the absence of the headteacher, are not left wondering what to do. It forestalls ill-considered personal judgements that may not be in the best interests of the school community and replaces *ad hoc* decision making with assurance and calmness. A managed response creates awareness that someone is taking control. School communities need that safety and security.

Is a management plan possible and necessary?

What do heads say?

There are so many things going on at once, it is essential to have a checklist where you can say 'we have done that', 'we have thought of this', it gives a sense of control. You lose time if you are sitting there for five minutes think-ing how you will respond. It gives you a place to start.

(Joshua, headteacher for 10 years)

I would argue very strongly that having a policy is not a hindrance. I really can't emphasize enough the importance of having a plan, I think to have . . . not so much for yourself because you know how you'll respond, but it's to help the senior staff on whom you would rely to help you carry the school community. It is their security really, for them to have the confidence that they know they will be able to deal with it . . . to know they have YOUR [Lily's emphasis] confidence that they will be able to help people to do things that they may not otherwise have done.

(Lily, headteacher for 5 years)

A team plan allows you in some ways to de-escalate the emotional tone and deal with the incident in the same structured way other things are managed in the school.

(Sean, headteacher for 10 years)

The last thing you want is senior staff in panic. If they panic, then your other staff panic and the students panic.

(Mike, headteacher for 11 years)

It is sine qua non [essential].

(Andrew, headteacher for 16 years)

If critical incidents are perceived as an essential management priority for schools, what format should plans take? One headteacher in England was critical of the education system guidelines for the management of critical incidents. She saw them as *'very administrative and de-personalized, as though it is easy to go from A to B to C to D. It is not quite like that'* (Peggy, headteacher for 15 years). Critical incident management is more than a mechanical process of an emergency evacuation. It is a guide for action that is worked through methodically which accounts for technical and personal elements, as well as unexpected outcomes.

Preparing a summary, a checklist or a flow chart for easy reference is valuable in a plan, but this needs to be supported by other material and pre-planning: *'It has got to be very, very short, something which is almost fundamental practice and not a philosophical policy'* (David, headteacher for 25 years). If it is fundamental practice, it will contain agreed principles that a school team have articulated beforehand for their environment.

The developmental process for the plan needs to begin before the events occur. The process will involve dialogue about where people stand on issues and options for action and will result in a plan that has school ownership. Joshua articulated the importance of this and his role as headteacher in its development:

I think the leadership part is getting them to understand this is not just another paper chase. This is not just another requirement that the government is bringing in or the school is bringing in. But it is a part of the school that you need to get inside you and have it just sit there so that you know about it, you believe in it and you trust in it but that you have a little bit of fear because you know how serious it can be. I have to give authenticity to the whole thing.

Several headteachers articulated their perspective on leadership in their plan's development – initiating, supporting and using personal experiences to emphasize the plan's importance. One headteacher suggested the following strategy for planning: '*As part of your staff development, set aside a staff meeting or whatever and go through it and you say, "is this what we want if this happens?"'* (Robyn, headteacher for 3 years). Another described her positive risk management approach and the 'shared management' of it:

As a principal [headteacher] I have tried to see where the issues may arise, so I try to eliminate bushfires as soon as a little brush fire starts, I deal with it now. It is my aim to remain calm so everybody knows what is going on. It is a joint effort instead of just me.

(Donna, headteacher for 6 years)

It is recommended that the two sides to the management of an incident, the technical and the personal, need to be attended to concurrently. For some incidents, however, one aspect will have precedence. Emily, a primary school headteacher, recounted her experience of managing a knife-wielding student who had threatened a teacher in front of the class. She did not focus immediately on 'step 1' of the system's critical incident management policy, but rather:

. . . it [management] varies so much . . . like in the knife attack, I had to get the boy secure so that everyone would be safe . . . I know you are supposed to notify the education system as step 1 but my real job was to make sure everyone was safe. So I don't care what the department says in terms of its steps, I know morally what I have to do is to make sure the rest of the kids are safe. Yeah, I am not going to follow the policy blindly.

(Emily, headteacher for 3 years)

When judging how to manage the 'personal' aspect, one executive staff member said: '*you look after the people who are most affected, then you go looking for a person who you think is least affected, because they also could be one of the ones who are most affected*' (Joshua, headteacher for 2 years).

Implementing a plan does more than manage the situation. It gives the school community confidence that senior staff are directing the situation for the best outcome for students, teachers, parents and the school. It minimizes inertia and provides a structure for people to go into 'automatic mode'.

The value of carrying out a review of a school's critical incident plan after an incident was highlighted by Andrew:

> *One of the things I guess I learnt from the experience was that the people that are most closely involved, like the counsellor, the chaplain and the deputy, find it particularly helpful to know that they can sit around the table with their friends and colleagues to just say, 'Well look, this is how I think it went'. Often just by reflecting on the process, they are able to deal with some of their own feelings which otherwise might get locked away.*
>
> (Andrew, headteacher for 16 years)

This proposition of 'reflecting on the plan' as a means of providing an opportunity to share feelings in a collegial environment is an important aspect of feeling in control.

But what happens if you don't have a plan? The experience of Felsham High School demonstrates the challenges faced by a school community where there had been little preparation for managing a critical incident. A student from the school was killed in a traffic accident and a friend was injured, in full view of many other students. The five members of the school administrative team took charge of the situation. Very concerned about a possible backlash from parents, they were intent 'to get this right'. They spent the day asking themselves *'Are we forgetting anybody? Is there any group we haven't notified?'* While they managed to get through the day, they overlooked contacting the part-time **school counsellor**.

Critical incident management

Reports from schools that indicate they have managed incidents well include four components that underpin effective processes. Responsible risk management for schools should include these four components. They are:

- a culture of proactive risk management to underpin school policies and procedures.
- the ability of the team to think things through, for example anticipating the spread of the impact of an event within a school and to other schools;

- an awareness of the need to balance competing interests and priorities, for example balancing the memorial service with the need for school routine, thus enabling students to sit for an important exam;
- an appreciation of the importance of 'timing', of when to initiate and when to hold back, for example when and how a primary class might be ready to remove a dead student's books and pens and use their desk.

Critical incidents upset the normal routines of the school that provide safety, predictability and accountability for students' whereabouts. In managing a critical incident, a balance needs to be achieved in changing the routine to meet the demands of the situation and the needs of the people involved and maintaining 'normality'. This does not mean the English lesson goes on as normal, but that the routine of the school facilitates the management process. The classroom can be used for discussion and support activities, such as creating condolence cards, planning memorials or producing a memory book. Depending on the teacher, the students and the enduring impact of the event, times can be set aside within lessons. Creating the balance between routine and change could be achieved by allowing the processing of reactions as they arise within a usual lesson format. Paul described how this occurred: *'If it interrupted the normal process of their science or math class, it was OK to give the students opportunities to talk about it'* (Paul, headteacher for 29 years). Using this approach allows teachers to maintain the essence of their instructive roles without feeling they are being expected to be therapists. It provides the opportunity for existing supportive relationships between teachers and their students to be utilized. Achieving a balance is not without its critics. Bernadette recounts:

> I would have been criticized in the past for getting back to normality too soon, asking students to go back to class when some of them could not go back to class, making an exception for the few and asking the majority to go back. People now understand that that is a much better way of going about it, because they have seen it happen and they have seen the normality begin to occur and they've seen the hype of those on the fringe settle down. So I think once they see reason, they are able to accept it.
>
> (Bernadette, headteacher for 12 years)

There are many factors that influence the decisions made, although practices used in the past can automatically be adopted without judging their suitability for the current event. This is where school leaders can exercise careful judgement and explain to the school community the path being taken; senior staff can verbalize reasons for particular actions. The concerns of staff should not be dismissed and differing viewpoints should be acknowledged. Although it is unlikely all will agree, they will be aware of the factors influencing the decision making.

Models of management

Schools and school systems have adopted different models for management of critical incidents depending on the availability of education system consultants and health and welfare services, geographic remoteness, financial constraints and specific school characteristics. The use of crisis response teams in a centralized or decentralized model (Johnson 1993) has advantages and disadvantages. Three main models of management are examined here, although there are many possible combinations of these. Each of the models includes 'outside help' of some form. Some schools might manage incidents 'in house', but because of the variety and sometimes complexity of critical incidents, 'checking' with an outside agency is recommended as quality practice. My own research indicates that, as a suggested minimum in managing incidents, headteachers should talk things through with a colleague, particularly in remote geographic areas where there are few services. The models described here are not the only ones possible; they have been chosen to exemplify the range of possible approaches:

- School critical incident management team with outside support where needed.
- School executive team plus designated local emergency team as part of education or health and welfare designated service.
- Outside team taking responsibility and reporting to the headteacher.

The effective processes mentioned previously need to be in operation irrespective of the model used. With each of these models, personnel are involved who are not normally part of the school's functioning. More details about the functioning of this association are described in Chapter 9.

School critical incident management team

Several benefits are to be gained from schools being proactive in the development of teams to manage critical incidents. The school executive structure may already have well-developed decision-making processes with different styles of problem identification and management being utilized. The existing roles of school personnel – for example, a year adviser or coordinator who has regular contact with parents of a particular age cohort – may be invaluable in acting as the link between the school and the parent group. Similarly, the management of school routines is second nature for deputies and heads of divisions. A school counsellor or the school's **educational psychologist** is already known to students. An invaluable advantage that these school personnel offer is that they know the students, the school routines and history and the wider school community. Additionally, by pre-planning as a team and through shared professional development experiences, trust and ownership will have been developed. It forestalls the experience recounted by Paul:

> So I had to do everything from managing the media, to preparing the staff to counsel and work to help the students, to working with the families, to planning the memorial services – a very challenging process.
>
> (Paul, headteacher for 29 years)

Although a staff member may be designated a 'pastoral care role', there may be different levels of expertise within any group of people. Some may be more skilled in supporting young people in crisis. Hence allocating a responsibility to someone in an existing role may not make the best use of the skills of available personnel, for example identifying who has the skills to be the liaison person with the media.

School executive team plus designated local emergency team

Johnson (1993) advocated that a team of professionals from a central education authority or specialist agency should come in to support the school. This support could range from the local emergency team taking control, to a few trained people who offer specialized counselling working alongside a school team.

Outside emergency personnel with headteacher

This model of management involves the headteacher taking responsibility for decision making with an outside expert attached to the school or available by telephone. It could also be a couple of staff members making decisions with outside people acting as critical friends.

The advantages and disadvantages of different models should be taken into account. Although schools recognize the value of 'outside help', the extent to which this may assist their management is based on several factors: the 'trust' the school team has in 'outsiders'; the familiarity of outside helpers with the school; the existence of a capable school team; and the incident. These issues are explored in detail in Chapter 9.

Availability of information

Information sharing is a key strategy for the management of critical incidents (Rowling 1999). As well as having a functional purpose, it also achieves other important outcomes. Information sharing can help allay fears, minimize rumours, forestall hysteria, fulfil duty of care responsibilities, create a sense of community and convey a sense of respect and caring. It is a concrete demonstration of school philosophy and practices and also contributes to risk management processes. On the other hand, withholding the truth can fuel a critical incident. Information about a critical incident allows people to 'complete an experience', so that they can begin to see it in its broader context as having occurred in the past (Robinson 2000). Schools who have effectively managed critical incidents emphasize the initial and ongoing importance of information flow. Doug, in describing his school's strategy over the weekend after a senior student had committed suicide on the Friday night, stated:

> *On Saturday, the response involved the principal [headteacher] and the deputy phoning all the senior staff. They were brought in for a meeting. A team of counsellors was there on the Sunday. Together they worked out with the staff what they would do with the students on the following day. Letters were prepared. The principal [headteacher] was involved in what would go into the letter but was not responsible for driving it. That was left to the deputy and one other person. The year coordinator's role was working with year groups and facilitating meetings with counsellors. We did not know what we would face. On Monday morning, we had a staff meeting immediately with the whole staff. The students then went to roll call classes, the teachers had a script of what to say, counsellors went with those teachers who felt they could not give the information unsupported. The same message went everywhere and I think that was important and it was a very simple and very clear message. The hysteria did not get out of control and I think perhaps it could have done.*
>
> (Doug, headteacher for 5 years)

In some circumstances, there may be a need for ongoing communication: when a student is in hospital on a critical list, a court case is involved, or many staff are affected, such as a colleague being arrested on suspected abuse.

Information gathering may be necessary, for example, about those who are already grieving due to a death in the family. The existing grief can be intensified by a school incident. The timing of information giving and the type and amount of information can be important if, for example, students are sitting for final exams.

Rumours can inflame critical incidents:

> *We as a school did a corporate restatement in a chapel service. We used it as an opportunity to remove a lot of the exaggeration of the story. Kids had been adding a touch of horror to it, becoming quite graphic and colourful. So we had a formal follow up and said, 'This is the truth'.*
>
> (Joshua, headteacher for 2 years)

Then you are dealing with the rumours that start up as to why the kids were on the cliffs, they are obviously out of their heads on alcohol or marijuana or something, not just two boys skylarking around and an accident happened. We also had a member of staff killed. He was killed very gruesomely in a car, sitting in his car on Butta Road. He died at the wheel. A truck just ploughed into the stationary cars. Well, by the time that had gone around the school community, students had not seen it but they knew it was gory, the moment they knew it was gory, it developed out of all proportion.

(Sean, headteacher for 10 years)

We told THE TRUTH [Hazel's emphasis] to the students and we told them how to access support and we tried to help them predict what would happen. The students were marvellous. The rumour mill didn't explode in the school. It was 'Alright they told us what's happening and we will move on'. It was amazing! That strategy of telling people what you know, not hiding it. Updating them, being truthful from the outset. And trying to help them predict what will happen next, creates some sense of surety of what might happen. And laying out who is available and how they get help. Those are themes in how we respond to crisis.

(Hazel, headteacher for 10 years)

Outside helpers are invaluable credible sources of technical information; for example, if there is a threat of the spread of an infectious disease and parents are requesting information or if there may be complications because of mass immunization. They may also be useful as conveyors of bad news, as the person who delivers bad news often becomes associated with it, hampering the development of a supportive relationship. In this instance, the school staff member called upon to provide ongoing support is at hand but the outside helper gives the news.

Not only is the flow of information important, but the mechanisms for the exchange of information vary. Letters to parents may need to be translated into many languages, staff briefings may need to take a structured format and student briefings may be required at a tutor group or class level, among age groups or, in some instances, in a whole school assembly. Decisions about these mechanisms need to be based on each school's structures, the nature of the incident, the skills and comfort of staff, and the purposes to be achieved in the information giving. For example, should information be given to small groups to forestall hysteria, or to everyone to ensure they all get the same message? Thinking about the process of information flow is critical in pre-planning and reflecting on incidents. Thus, making an announcement in the school break requires ensuring that staff on duty in the playground get the same information. Also, teachers need to be identified who will require support while telling their class. Similarly, when students are on a excursion, provision has to be made for information exchange:

> *The change in our practice that followed was the way in which we think about communicating with the school when we have a group of students away from the school. We learned that we hadn't thought about the worst case scenarios of when we might send students away; how would anyone contact us back here at the school? We made a change in how we plan for any kind of field trip. We created small cards, small wallet-size cards for all the supervisors going on a trip that contained the Central Education body's security phone number. That is manned 24 hours a day, so they could always get through to someone to talk about their problem and they could phone the right people. We haven't had to use that, but it is a way of ensuring teachers can always reach someone.*
>
> (Hazel, headteacher for 10 years)

Information exchange is also important between the school and the education system. For example, if the education system obtains information from the police, this needs to be passed on to school personnel instantly, so that rumours spreading among the local community are not their only source of information.

Intensive or adverse media coverage

> *One is much more conscious of the role that is played by the media in such events today and this has caused a growing consciousness on our part for me to ensure that processes are in place and that people need protection, if you like.*
>
> (Bernadette, headteacher for 12 years)

Coping with the media is a vital aspect of school management, especially management of a critical incident. Previous negative media coverage can influence a school to either ignore media demands for information or sensitize staff to the need for controlling media hype in reporting a critical incident. This control can be achieved by giving the media accurate information. Society's views about education are increasingly being shaped by media reporting about schools. Critical incidents provide the media with an opportunity for challenging schools' performance, particularly in relation to duty of care. For example:

> *With Bruce's death, there were more serious duty of care implications because one of the papers got hold of the idea that it was a punishment run, that he had been made to go on this early morning run because he had been*

naughty. And that was not helpful. The idiot reporter said he was there as a boarder 20 years ago and punishment runs were a regular part of the programme, all this sort of . . . pretty unhealthy for a while. The media are pretty cruel to boarding schools anyway.

(Andrew, headteacher for 16 years)

Similarly, Brian recounted his experience:

The press tried to. The press . . . one element of the press, one particular local newspaper and one particular female reporter wanted to stir it up. She digs, she digs a knife in. This was an excellent opportunity for her and she turned up with a photographer several times wanting to come in and we wouldn't allow her to. That annoyed her. Her reporting was all head to head – 'Death at school, These are the questions we should be asking, Are our children safe?' Things like that. We felt that was an attack on us. Even with the Mum, she was almost getting the Mum to say, almost advising the Mum on what route she should be taking, the legal route for compensation, whereas other parts of the local press were very responsible: 'This is what happened, this is what the school spokesperson said, this is what a spokesperson for the family said'.

(Brian, headteacher for 9 years)

It is also imprudent to ignore media requests. Rather than saying 'no comment' and denying the press access, it generally suffices to give them controlled access and provide them with just the factual information. They do not actually go away, but it can provide you with the time and space to act.

Geoffrey thought very carefully about the visual image of an interview:

I refused to speak to the media, because of their glorification of the damage approach. I said I would speak to them on the day the building reopens. I didn't want my photograph taken in front of a burnt out building. I said this to staff and they agreed. That is a principle of mine.

(Geoffrey, headteacher for 15 years)

The intrusiveness of the media worried many headteachers: *'their walking into the school and cheating in the way they covered the story and got their information'* (Paul, headteacher for 29 years).

Not all experiences are negative. Some headteachers do respond to the media's request for interviews with positive outcomes:

I must say that the interviewer with whom I dealt was quite sensitive. I quickly established the facts and I made it very clear the standpoint we took. At that time, I tried to contain the supposition, I gave them the facts. I had felt that if I did not give them an interview, they would come and be more aggressive than if one cooperated with them in a reasonable manner. Establish the facts. Having done that, we weren't being bothered by them again. I do think that turned out to be a better move.

(Bernadette, headteacher for 12 years)

Care needs to be taken when talking with the media. For example, a headteacher threatened with closure of his school is placed in a difficult position. Villa recalls:

*I realized I had to be very careful because I had been approached by the newspapers and TV. So at first I were very, very careful, very wary, I blocked everything but later on I established quite a good rapport with the local paper and they did a series of articles which were favourable to us and the school, but not attacking the **LEA**, which obviously I could not do.*

(Villa, acting headteacher for 3 years)

The nature of the event

There are some events – deaths, intruders in the school, fires or a teacher accused of abuse – that can be classified as critical incidents, either when they occur or because of the impact of some of the factors previously identified. Additionally, a cumulatively stressful event can occur after responses to several events in a short time. None of these events has to be major, but they can build collectively in a synergetic way to create the same impact as a critical incident.

Controversy about critical incident stress debriefing

The focus of this book is school communities and a discussion of debriefing sits within that context. School culture is an important element in identifying existing prescriptions for behaviour and rituals within the school environment. When debriefing after a critical incident, practices are shaped by occupational health issues, religious beliefs, the school ethos and history, as well as the other factors identified earlier in this chapter.

Many issues complicate the debriefing after a critical incident. Raphael and Wilson (2000) present a comprehensive review of the issues, which include: who should be debriefed, who is stressed or traumatized; the context for the debriefing and when it should take place; the purpose of debriefing – catharsis, the prevention of mental health or workplace problems, the prevention of post-traumatic stress; the form the debriefing should take – talking through, a structured confrontational or non-confrontational approach. There may be a range of care options, with brief support interventions, such as psychological first aid, education and information, group support, focused counselling and practical assistance. Some of these are natural human processes that already exist to some extent in schools and do not require professional support from outside the school, whereas others are relatively new and have not been evaluated. It is important that the pre-existing natural support mechanisms are not abandoned in favour of expert helpers. In the main, knowledge about critical incident management for schools has been adapted from work with emergency service personnel – that is, people who are likely to experience stress and trauma in their work lives. Although critical incident debriefing should be part of a larger intervention framework, it has not been evaluated in this context. As debriefing is likely to be provided by personnel from outside the school, it is discussed in more detail in Chapter 9.

Short- and long-term issues related to critical incidents

Rituals and memorials

Careful decision making needs to be taken about the timing and type of a memorial or ritual. Ben talked about how his school performed a ritual when a member of the community took a student hostage:

> We had not so much an exorcism, that's not the right word, but a reclaiming ceremony, a religious reclaiming ceremony. It was done quite deliberately. The parish priest came and carried a light and walked around saying, 'this is our safe school'. It was making it safe.
>
> (Ben, year 11 student aged 16 years)

Triggers

The ability to anticipate incidents that trigger a reaction from students is important both in the short and long term. Paul recalled how the media kept bringing the event back to consciousness: 'They always wanted to come back, to do a follow-up, asking "How are they doing a month after?" If there is a parallel incident somewhere else, then they will come back again' (Paul, headteacher for 29 years). Anniversaries or marker events such as graduations can preoccupy students. School routines may trigger a response from students. At Columbine High School, it was the fire bell that sounded to warn of the danger. After the event, the tone of the bell was changed so that it did not trigger flashbacks.

If a group or class has had the misfortune to have experienced more than one event, they may view themselves as being cursed or jinxed. This can result in students waiting for the next event, with fatalistic explanations being adopted or 'out of control' behaviour involving increased risk taking. Acknowledging the fear and increasing young people's control and predictability in a secure environment may assist in overcoming the fear.

Positive outcome from planning

Changed practice in the management of critical incidents has already occurred in many countries. Sean, a headteacher in Australia, recounts:

> *Because we had everything in place, the whole thing was handled at a much better level. We could talk on assemblies about it, we could talk to individuals, we expected grief and therefore could handle grief. We ourselves were grieving and could handle grieving and also some of the staff were affected because the students were very, very popular. I think the better handling of it was related to a paradigm shift in the thinking of the administration of the school, how are we going to do this?*
>
> (Sean, headteacher for 10 years)

Villa recalls the experience of a critical incident in England in the 1970s:

> *It was like treading water in the dark because you did not know what to do or say. As soon as you made a telephone call and said, 'Your child has been involved in the accident', before you could get out 'but nobody is injured very badly', there would be screams on the other end of the phone. That was the thing that affected me at the time I remember. Afterwards, I wondered what would have been the best way of breaking the news?*
>
> (Villa, acting headteacher for 3 years)

Conclusion

This chapter has documented experiences that need to be considered by all school communities. Drawing from school members' experiences, generalizations about quality practice can be identified to improve management in the future. This is not meant to convey that there is only one way of acting – decisions need to be made to suit the event and the school community. It is important to accept that mistakes will be made and that there will be unforeseen consequences, such as legal proceedings.

In trying to make sense of the incident, people will want to apportion blame. This is a natural reaction. A challenge for schools is to manage the anger and fear that results from traumatic events. This is the case in particular for survivors whose reactions are compounded by the guilt they experience.

If a critical incident happens in or near a school, it is the learning and working environment that is violated, so both students and staff need to be a focus. The perceived benefits of school community management of a critical incident are changes in perception of self and the school, improved interpersonal relationships and a changed view of life. A critical incident can strengthen a school's sense of community.

Implications for practice

- Critical incident management plans should guide action and account for unexpected outcomes, technical elements and personal elements.
- Community members need to be involved in the development of the plan so that the whole school has ownership of it.
- Implementation of the critical incident management plan can give the school community confidence in senior staff.
- The key components of responsible risk management outlined on page 66 need to be considered when developing or reviewing a critical incident management plan.
- Senior staff need to keep the school community informed about reasons why particular actions have been taken during a critical incident.
- Ensure accurate information is provided – rumours can inflame a critical incident.
- Media requests can be effectively managed by controlling access to the media and providing them with factual information.
- Many issues are associated with debriefing. It is important that any debriefing is carried out by someone with the necessary skills.
- It is important to identify potential triggers that may prompt flashbacks to previous traumatic events and implement strategies to either eliminate or manage them.

Further reading

Johnson, K. (1993) *School Crisis Management: A Hands on Guide for Training Crisis Response Teams*. Alameda, CA: Hunter House.
Klicker, R.L. (2000) *A Student Dies, a School Mourns*. Philadelphia, PA: Taylor & Francis.

Petersen, S. and Straub, R.L. (1992) *School Crisis Survival Guide: Management Techniques and Materials for Counsellors and Administrators*. West Nyack, NY: Centre for Applied Research in Education.

Raphael, B. and Wilson, J.P. (2000) *Psychological Debriefing: Theory, Practice and Evidence*. New York: Cambridge University Press.

Yule, W. and Gold, A. (1993) *Wise Before the Event: Coping with Crises in Schools*. London: Calouste Gulbenkian Foundation.

CHAPTER 6

Supportive school environment

Introduction

There is evidence of a link between social support and health (Stroebe 2000). This provides a theoretical basis for the potential positive impact of a supportive school environment on young people's experience of loss. Social support is a complex phenomenon, but it is seen to have a buffering effect on psychosocial transitions or stressful life events (Cohen and Syme 1985). A deficit in social support has been associated with poor health in the first year of bereavement (Raphael 1985) and poor outcomes for psychological trauma (Mitchell and Everly 2000). A study of late adolescent college age students (LaGrande 1988) found that, next to personal resources, social support was the single most potent force in recovering from relationship losses. Similarly, in a study of 12- to 19-year-olds, Gray (1989) found that high informal social support following a personal loss helped reduce depression.

Symbolic interactionism, another theoretical construct (Berger and Luckman 1967), helps to explain the processes at work in our social interactions. Rosenblatt (1988) believes this theory helps us to understand the importance of others in defining ourselves and our circumstances. Young people look to their peers and teachers in their social environments for support to help define the reality of their loss, to help express feelings associated with it and to assist in integrating the experience into their lives. The school as an institution can provide an environment (in terms of programmes, practices and policies) that is supportive as well as being the location from which individuals can provide assistance. Petersen and Straub (1992) suggested that a consequence of a school community that does not support a young person at a time of crisis can be a lack of connectedness by the student with the school. Furthermore, this supportive environment is necessary because classroom curricula might encourage the expression of thoughts and feelings about grief, while social pressures might work against it. That is, if another teacher tells the students to 'pull themselves together', the impact of curricula will be limited.

Rutter (1995) noted that positive influences in the environment help develop a sense of personal worth in students. This viewpoint emphasizes the centrality of the individual and represents one approach to understanding the relationship between schooling and personal and social health outcomes. Additionally, research on resilience has identified the dependability and availability of the school, the headteacher and staff as important elements in maintaining and strengthening young people's well-being (Benard 1995).

Broadly conceptualized, a supportive environment provides for many types of support: informational support by providing access to concrete facts and offering suggestions; esteem support by valuing the person's ability to adapt; network support by spending time with the person; instrumental support for students doing practical things like collecting class notes when a friend is absent from school; and emotional support by letting a friend talk about their experience (Cutrona *et al.* 1990).

The various forms of support are made up from a range of elements that create supportive personal and social school environments (Rowling and Burr 1997). These elements interact and overlap:

- the places in school settings: the classroom, the school buildings and environs, the **school climate** and the local area;
- the people: the students, teachers, other school staff, families, health and community workers;
- the processes and practices: decision making, participation, caring, information exchange;
- the policies involving the guidelines for action and for resource allocation;
- the programmes for coordinated learning in classrooms and across the school activities that occur.

However, it is not just these elements in isolation but their interrelationships, cooperation, compatibility and coherence that contribute to creating supportive environments (Rowling and Burr 1997). School communities are dynamic environments. Consequently, these elements need to be continually monitored and reviewed to identify their current relevance and effectiveness.

Places

The 'places' that can be supportive for young people in schools include the classroom, other school buildings and their surroundings and the local area. These are places identified by a physical structure, but there is also the school climate, a supportive psychosocial environment that provides social and personal safety.

Classroom

An atmosphere of personal safety needs to be created in the classroom for discussions about loss and grief, and for students returning to class after a death in the family or other major loss. The classroom also needs to be free from 'teasing', either because of the different life circumstances in a child's family or because of a child's physical difference due to a serious illness or disability.

School buildings

School buildings and their environs need to offer quiet spaces for small peer groups who wish to talk or for individuals seeking some quiet corner. Often the school library provides this haven. Private space, out of view of other students, should be available for meetings between the school psychologist, pastoral care staff and students. This ensures confidentiality and allows talking to take place without interruption.

Where the school environment has been violated, rituals of 'reclaiming place' can help restore feelings of personal safety. Matt described the feeling he had when he walked into his school grounds after a young man unconnected to the school had hanged himself in the playground:

I walked into the place and it was just like a leaden atmosphere had come across the whole place, it was just extraordinary, it was like a graveyard. It is normally a buoyant, vibrant place. People have said they walk into the place and they can just tell it is a really lovely child-centred, warm, happy place. But it was terrible! The staff were just sobbing in their classrooms and they had kids there. It was just an absolute mess. They were angry that someone had taken over their bit of turf. I believe that you have to put a lot of emotional energy into a place to get it how you want it to be for the children. There is a wonderful ownership by the staff of the school, they are extremely committed people. They felt very, very intruded upon. And the gravity of having someone commit suicide where you spend a lot of your time pumping emotional energy into, it is very, very difficult. Adults had to reclaim the place for the kids and that was my role to start the process of reclaiming the place for the school community.

(Matt, headteacher for 17 years)

Matt undertook this process by providing ongoing support for students and staff, focusing on their sense of safety. A 'reclaiming ceremony' also took place.

School climate

The school climate, ethos or psychosocial environment is one of the most difficult areas to define, but it has a powerful effect on creating an atmosphere that is supportive. It is identified with what 'our' school stands for.

Case study – Supportive school climate

Kair High School is a large multicultural comprehensive high school in the Sydney metropolitan area of New South Wales. It has approximately 120 teaching staff and about 1350 students, 75 per cent of whom come from **non-English-speaking backgrounds**. The school has a strong welfare structure supported by: a well-developed and frequently articulated 'philosophy' of welfare where energies are directed not only to the needs of students but also the needs of staff for support; leadership by people who have the ability to 'hold it all together in their head'; and many like-minded people who implement the philosophy and documented procedures. A key to the supportive environment is the practices (often not documented) that the elements previously defined are translated into, the ways of operating that have evolved out of trial and error in the implementation of the philosophy. These include: teachers acting as student advocates; time spent on information gathering and dissemination; problem posing and solving based on information exchange; flexibility in procedures in handling individual students; role modelling by staff; early intervention through perceptive problem identification with 'at risk' students and situations; and positive relationships between student/teacher, teacher/teacher, parent/teacher. All these factors interact to form an environment that is supportive of staff and students' personal and social needs. These elements were not easily identified in this school. It took the author a year of careful observation and probing questioning about observed practices to identify this ethos. It emerged from conversations with people in the school and from documents where certain words kept being repeated: 'care', 'respect', 'emphasizing the positive', 'support', 'approachability'. These words seemed to reflect the ethos of the school and, for many staff, the whole purpose of the school and their role in it, a sense of 'our' school.

A supportive school climate conveys that accepting help is okay. This is especially important for adolescents who need to know that seeking help is not shameful, a sign of immaturity or of being unable to cope.

Agreement by staff that this is the philosophy of the school is important, so that staff members whose beliefs may be different from this do not make belittling or sarcastic statements to students who do seek help.

Fred articulated what he saw as a supportive environment at the time of a critical incident:

Looking at the situation, that it moves along as it should in terms of the resources coming in and the support provided. Looking at all aspects of the communication of parents. Often times responding to the kinds of questions and concerns that teachers and children have, very openly and that there is a forum for that. There is opportunity to talk, listening well and responding. There is a place for teachers to come to have sustenance, have some opportunity to meet their own needs and not feel that they have to continue on or that they are going to be judged in a certain way if they are not managing. It is being very aware of others' needs and that's a challenge!

(Fred, headteacher for 1 year)

The school climate is particularly important for the students and staff of a school that has been judged to have 'failed' to reach prescribed standards, or people in the local area see the school as poor and run-down, with staff who are uncaring and unable to impose discipline. With this backdrop, a school that experiences a critical incident may be less 'resilient'. It may not have the elements of a supportive environment identified in its places, people, policies, practices and programmes, or the support of members of the local community. It may even be inferred that the school's existing state contributed to the incident. Geoffrey and Max both experienced this:

We were trying to build up the image of the school. I didn't want people to see this as a poor run-down area where someone was dissatisfied with the school so they wanted to burn it down. This wasn't the case.

(Geoffrey, headteacher for 15 years)

This school was in special measures. It was a failing school a couple of year's ago. We pulled the school out of special measure in a year and a half, which is no mean feat, but you then have the difficulty of keeping the ball rolling. You are a failing school if you don't get high grades, which ignores the reality of the quality of pupils you are getting here in terms of academic ability. So there is that backdrop. It just appeared to be one thing after another [with the number of critical incidents].

(Max, headteacher for 1 year)

Both these headteachers indicated that being publicly judged for poor academic achievement or discipline created a vulnerability that added to difficulties in handling a critical incident. The image of the school has be identified as a having a symbolic meaning in the health of the community (MacIntyre and Ellaway 1999), both as locations for community activities and as perceived barometers of the state of the community.

People

People with direct links to the school are easily identifiable, but the range of people who consider themselves to be connected to a school is dependent on physical location, school history and culture, the strength of the alumni organization and formal links with business and community health and welfare agencies. This wider community can also include neighbouring schools. It is essential that communication is maintained with nearby schools if one school has experienced a critical incident. Students may have siblings and friends in other schools, and adolescents may work with young people from other schools in the locality, so students in another school can be greatly affected even though the incident occurred elsewhere. Communication will be particularly important if the incident is a suicide. The actions of a senior college demonstrate their concept of the school community and how they actively created support within that community.

Case study – A continuing community

Mt. Loosley Senior College educated young people for the last two years of secondary school. Staff were concerned about the incidence of suicide in the area. Although none of their students had committed suicide at school, two former students had taken their lives. Staff felt being at school protected the students in some way. For example, there were cut-out outlines of hands around the school with the words 'Do you need a helping hand?', with information about where to get various types of assistance. They wanted to extend practices like this. They formed the idea of a 'Continuing Community'. Although the students were at school, the welfare team worked to form seamless links between the school and the local health and welfare agency personnel. These people came into the school for special 'health fairs' and were encouraged to conduct extra-curricular sessions with students. The hope was that with this personal engagement with outside groups, the students might be more prepared to access their services once they left school. Welfare staff in the school met every three months with the outside groups. This provided an opportunity for the teams to coordinate and work together as well as link with the school. The school welfare team also encouraged the formation of an active Alumni Association. One of the functions of this was to provide a mechanism for former students to be involved with current students in extra-curricular activities, such as building and racing solar energy vehicles. A crucial connection that was emphasized continually by the welfare team to the rest of the school community was that the school climate being created supported the learning of students and the working environment of staff.

In developing their critical incident management plan, another school invited community agencies, including the police, community health and welfare agencies, to nominate representatives to be members of the committee that was developing the plan. Not only did these people provide expertise and a different viewpoint, but their presence in the school allowed them to familiarize themselves with the personnel, structures and procedures of the school. Consequently, in time of emergency, they would know who to deal with and the existing procedures that could be utilized.

Local education authorities also have personnel who might be invaluable during a critical incident. The critical incident in Brian's school was so overwhelming and created such controversy that help from the education authority was sought:

When I made the first phone call [to the LEA] I said, 'I want someone to deal with the press because I am not going to' and neither was anyone else in school. We have a policy that only the headteacher can talk to the press anyway. I was not going to and the LEA were very good at managing the press.

(Brian, headteacher for 9 years)

In a supportive school environment, diversity is acknowledged and all students are valued. Adolescents often look to their peers for support and fostering the skills of young people to be supportive is a valuable preventive approach. Formal peer support programmes can strengthen natural helping, but adolescents can take on 'the grief of the world', so care needs to be exercised in encouraging them to be supportive and in identifying limits to their responsibilities.

People can provide support in a variety of ways but emotional support is the most common. For young people who do not feel comfortable talking about the loss, they can be encouraged to be supportive by being with their friend, asking if the friend will help them choose new clothes or offering to help them with their schoolwork.

All staff in a school need to be supportive of children and adolescents who are grieving. At a minimal level this involves being non-judgemental, attentive listening and keeping students' personal information private (see Chapter 8).

Process and practices

'Support is embedded in the daily processes of social life' (Leatham and Duck 1990: 21). These processes include participation by school community members, thereby affirming teachers', students' and parents' basic rights to be included in the programmes and practices about loss and grief in their environment. Involvement in the decision-making process needs to take place in a truly participatory way, so that students are supported in designing and conducting memorial services or rituals that mark endings and beginnings. This contribution by students needs to be respected and valued. Similarly, parents need to be involved in any decision making about school participation in funerals and grief support activities. The type and placement of memorials in a school should be carefully considered, especially if the death being commemorated was traumatic. In this case, individuals traumatized by the event may not wish to have constant reminders (Klicker 2000).

A supportive school environment has well-developed processes for identifying children at risk. These processes are followed through with practices that suit the young person's needs and wishes. This requires an effective pastoral care system in which staff are trained and supported to carry out their role, a role that is valued by the whole school community. Jill articulates what she sees as being necessary from a student's perspective:

What does help is if the students feel there is at least one adult that they can relate to. That helps the situation, regardless of who that adult is. I would hope that there are none, but there probably are students who would not feel comfortable in being able to go to an adult and say, 'this is how I feel at this time in a critical incident or at any stage'. [I would like] to think that they have a reasonable amount of confidence that they would be listened to and heard.

(Jill, deputy headteacher for 3 years)

Pastoral care practices should not only be informal, but be articulated in school procedures. These procedures for support in schools can have a profound effect on the mental health of students and staff (Galloway 1990). For both groups, welfare structures and practices need to be prominent, reviewed continuously for effectiveness and exist as an integral part of the purpose of the school. Andrew described this as follows: '*The pastoral network is activated straight away so that the kids know that if they need support or help, they know that they go to the person that they would normally go to*' (Andrew, headteacher for 16 years). Welfare is not a separate part of the school.

Bernadette acknowledged the need to accommodate individual needs in supporting grieving students and to provide for that in the school's strategies:

So we would not have a situation, for example, where in putting some supportive structure in place, we would not just herd everyone in and say, 'Well we are going to take this time for prayer now, we will do it all together and you will all have to do it'. It is much more likely that structured situations would be set up in a way that offered them freedom of choice on how they might like to be with their friends while they are grieving over a fellow student or other incident.

(Bernadette, headteacher for 12 years)

The portrayal of how relationships end and the acknowledgement of the pain of grief can be demonstrated if the critical incident involves the death of a student or staff member. For example, involvement of students in a funeral not only provides opportunities for students' expression of respect and caring, but also helps to acquaint them with a family's grief. Actions taken by the school community at the time of the death of one of their members indicate to all that a loss has occurred. When no actions are taken, the message is conveyed that the school member is not important and the school leaders are insensitive or inexperienced. Action should not just be a passive agreement to a memorial service and attendance by school leaders, but the demonstration of care. Leadership in expression of grief helps individuals and the school as an organization create meaning out of loss experiences.

Creative rituals and rites have the power to comfort both secular and school communities with relatively heterogeneous belief systems. They make the values of the school community explicit. Members of the school community also need to be informed of the rituals participated in on their behalf. This will help the rituals to be perceived as being helpful, thus affirming their value.

Other practices in supportive schools concern student safety, including care with student movement to and from and around the school, regular practice of evacuation procedures and foresight in planning for accidents in sporting venues and on excursions. Supportive school environments also have in place practices that demonstrate concern for staff stress due to grief experiences. This is discussed in Chapter 4.

Policies

Involvement in the policy decision-making process needs to be truly participatory, from the initiation of the development of new policies to their implementation. The most significant procedural policy for loss and grief is the school's critical incident management plan. The development of this plan is not only important for awareness raising and creating a sense of ownership, but it also provides the opportunity to accommodate the distinctive culture of each school. Fitting the management of incidents in with a school's philosophy and its system of beliefs and getting things in the right proportion for each school community is an important priority. It provides the scope each school requires to focus on meeting the needs of their students, their families and the staff rather than following mechanical de-personalized and de-contextualized actions.

Case studies – Developing a plan

Mountview High School was operating a 'Healthy Schools Committee' as part of its health-promoting school activity (Chapter 1), so the process for creating the plan was put under that umbrella. There were several committees – staff welfare, student welfare, canteen policy and gender equity. Each sub-committee was represented on the umbrella group. Staff were represented on all committees and students on all except staff welfare. The critical incident committee came under the same structure, so it also had staff representation and, perhaps crucially, non-teaching staff representation as well.

Kair High School included parent representation on its critical incident management plan committee. The parent involved was also a palliative care nurse, who brought her expertise to the committee. This enhanced the parent and professional community links. This parent led the discussion at the school council meeting with other parents about the plan.

Other policies that are important in the management of loss and grief are provisions for the privacy of student information and school procedures around violence. Schools should be a place where violence towards teachers, whether physical or verbal, is acted upon swiftly and where the welfare of staff and students is a paramount concern within the context of well-developed discipline and occupational health and safety policies.

Programmes

Formal curricula for young people about loss and grief is detailed in Chapter 4, but all school community members need education about grief – teachers, school administrative staff and parents. In addition, welfare staff in secondary schools need familiarity with youth suicide, an issue addressed in Chapter 11. Extra-curricular programmes that provide for the diversity of students' interests and abilities can contribute to the maintenance of feelings of self-worth for grieving students. They also provide the opportunity for students to connect with adults in less formal settings. This may contribute to the support a student perceives is available.

Conclusion

Although the grief experiences of young people or of a critical incident in a school can be seen as negative, the positive actions and environments already in place in schools should be commended. A focus on the healing environment a school provides can shift the negative orientation of painful experiences to one that is positive and provides opportunities for the growth of individuals and the strengthening of the school community.

Implications for practice

- Create a classroom atmosphere where students feel safe and secure.
- Create places where students can go to take 'time out' when they need it and where student confidentiality can be maintained to encourage them to seek and access help.
- It is important that all staff support the philosophy that accepting help is okay.
- Maintain effective communication with nearby schools in the event of a critical incident.
- Identify personnel from local community agencies to provide the school with support after a critical incident.
- All school community members need to have the opportunity to participate in decision making relating to programmes and practices about loss and grief in their school.
- Establish formal processes to identify students at risk.
- Pastoral care practices need to be embedded in school procedures and regularly reviewed.
- Establish or review the school's critical incident management plan to ensure loss and grief is managed proactively and the harm associated with the incident is minimized.
- All school community members need education about loss and grief.

Further reading

Galloway, D. (1990) *Pupil Welfare and Counselling: An Approach to Personal and Social Education across the Curriculum*. London: Longman.

Rowling, L. and Burr, A. (1997) Creating supportive environments, in D. Colquhoun, K. Goltz and M. Sheehan (eds) *The Health Promoting School: Policy, Programmes and Practice in Australia*. Marrickville: Harcourt Brace.

Sheehan, M., Marshall, B., Cahill, H., Rowling, L. and Holdsworth, R. (2000) *SchoolMatters: Mapping and Managing Mental Health in Schools*. Canberra: Commonwealth Department of Health and Aged Care (available at http://www.curriculum.edu.au/mindmatters).

CHAPTER 7

Being in charge

Softly, softly. Inside the school gates, 600 shocked pupils. Outside, press and politicians demanding answers. When tragedy strikes, how do headteachers cope.

(*The Guardian*, 5 December 2000)

I was talking to the boss of another school, and they lost a boy the other week, you are never quite the same after these incidents. You don't realize until you face it as a principal just what the loss of a young life actually means to you as a principal.

(Sean, headteacher for 10 years)

Introduction

The role of headteachers has changed over the last decade. Not only do they have to manage people and events, engender a culture in the school community that represents the shared vision and be an academic leader, they also have to be a business manager with liability insurance and legal and occupational health expertise. For a headteacher, management of grief involves many of these responsibilities. The grief experiences encountered include staff and students experiencing divorce or death, the death of a teacher, crises where staff or student safety is threatened, and critical incidents that affect school community members. In addition to managing the events and resultant emotional responses, headteachers may need to be aware of insurance liabilities (e.g. where the negligence of the school or an outside organization such as a bus company is at issue) or to have legal knowledge about court proceedings if there is an inquest. These multiple demands are in large part due to increasing educational and societal pressures on schools and increased accountability requirements.

Irrespective of headteachers' leadership styles, personal and professional challenges will be encountered in fulfilling their roles in this contentious and often emotionally charged area. Although this chapter places the headteacher 'centre stage', it does not mean 'the stage' is being ignored. Other chapters in this book focus on the stage, the other actors and the supportive environment. Educational administrators identify differing styles of leadership, but for many school community members the key influencing factor in leadership and management of grief experiences is the way the headteacher acts, speaks and makes decisions.

Challenges that arise from the educational and social context

Economic pressures in the 1990s have resulted in educational systems being downsized and streamlined. In some cases, this has meant withdrawing systemic consultant services, professionals whose 'products' were less well identifiable than an academic 'score', which is a criterion used for judging school performance. These professionals were often the support people for headteachers, their staff and the students' parents. They were professionals familiar with both the staff and the social and economic contexts in their districts. They were people who could readily be called upon for advice and assistance. Now there are fewer consultant services; the onus is on school personnel to actively seek them out, adding to existing demands on their time. The impact of this contraction of support services is clearly visible in the management of grief in school communities.

Legal issues are of increasing concern to schools and headteachers:

There is something about being an educator that is being lost in the legality issue. I am not quite sure how we address it. But I can tell you that is the biggest area of concern for me as a new principal. That legal preparation.
(Barney, headteacher for 1 year)

I now have a whole section in our staff manual on risk management policy. We just didn't use that language before. We are working through occupational health and safety and worker rehabilitation at the moment. You need a law degree to work it through. Most principals have not been trained, they have got to know their role by their shirt tails. They have no doubt gone on to study in areas of administration, but people are promoted on the basis of their teaching and not for organization or management skills. That is increasingly difficult.
(Bernadette, headteacher for 12 years)

As systems centralize or decentralize, the responsibility structure that identifies the person or group to whom the headteacher of a government-funded school is answerable can change. Whatever structure exists, the key issue is how supported the headteacher and staff feel by 'the system' or the 'governing body' and parents. Where legal proceedings are brought against a school that is part of an educational system, where the system itself is the insured and hence the subject of litigation, the perception of support by school staff and the need for sensitive handling from outside are critical. Such support includes providing advice to a headteacher and staff, for example 'don't make any admissions'. Additionally, legal professionals will need to be aware of the developmental level – both cognitive and emotional – of the students they interview. Headteachers were aware of the limited support that was available:

Central government over the last 18–20 years has been working towards the dismantling of the LEAs. Perhaps it not so much dismantling but reorganizing it, cutting it down, fine tuning it, making them more answerable. Nevertheless, services and budgets that were held for those services are now devolved to schools. So you have governing bodies plus the Head managing the school. They are the ones saying, 'that money buys this, that money buys that'. Depending on what sort of crank the head is [laughter]*, you can get different things happening at different schools. What has occurred is the recogniton of things called 'critical incidents', where there is a potential Lockerbie, bomb on site, armed intruder, they have realized it. What the LEA says is 'you must have a policy'. What I would like to see on major issues is the LEA have their policy, have agreed the policy with the school, have been fundamental in shaping that policy in the school and injecting into it whatever resources are available to them. Not saying 'you have a responsibility for a budget which is limited according to the number of pupils and out of that you have to purchase all help you need for critical incidents'. I would like to not have to worry if the school budget can buy enough supply staff in, so that I can say to colleagues 'you need to be off site for the day'. I want the system to take responsibility for what affects not just this school but the community. We are not getting that. And we won't get it. When I came back to the north, the school I was in was at the heart of a three-day gun siege. Every police officer had back-up police officers. They were taken off after so many hours, they had counselling. Not one LEA officer came to the school to see what was happening.*

(Peggy, headteacher for 15 years)

A caring word from above. That's all that is needed. A word that was not guarded or couched in terms of – 'hey there is nothing wrong there that I am going to find out is there?'

(Sean, headteacher for 10 years)

Headteachers are responsible to different groups, such as a governing body or a school council. These groups may be familiar with legal and management questions. To this context the headteacher brings the educational dimension. This is where clashes can occur, for while the council may have technical knowledge about grief in an organization, schools are organizations with different purposes that involve personal interchanges not product development. This element identifies a critical role for the headteacher in decision making about school management of loss and grief issues. Within a headteacher's educational organizational responsibility the core issues in the management of crises are: if the headteacher feels supported; if the educational implications they delineate are understood and acknowledged; and if they experience pressure and a sense that the 'buck stops here' but with no support.

Headteachers are keenly aware of their responsibility:

I was very clear about what my job was. It was not to make judgements about who was right or wrong, it was to manage the damage. To turn it around, move it forward if I could. It is a sense of responsibility. It is not a sense of isolation, because I did not feel isolated. I didn't feel that only I could do it. It wasn't heroic. It was 'this is where the rubber hits the road!' 'I am the one who has to manage this!' 'I'm the one who sets the tone'.

(Hazel, headteacher for 10 years)

I don't think you realize as a principal until someone dies under your care. Then it just clarifies in one awful period of time what your roles and responsibilities are to the community, individually and collectively.

(Janet, headteacher for 7 years)

Just the weight of responsibility, just being responsible for all these people, whether that is a realistic way of looking at your role, that's how I felt. That can be very, very wearing at times. You make a ridiculous mistake and you erode your bank account, it affects your relationship with your community.

(Matt, headteacher for 10 years)

There is a real problem in society with the image of the principal because there are a lot of people who have the idea that the principal is there to solve everything. No business operates at that level. No other management of any institution operates at that level, but there is this perception out there in the community that the principal is the person who solves everything . . . it is sort of like a god-like figure that steps in.

(Sean, headteacher for 10 years)

A critical incident can exemplify differing expectations of headteachers' responsibilities. They need to manage the incident, ideally through a school team, and to be confident that, between staff and outside people, everything that is needed is in place. This involves being clear on the formal procedures that are required statutorily by their educational systems and their governing bodies on such issues as health and safety. A full understanding of those requirements needs to be shared with everyone who works with them or is on the premises on a day-to-day basis. Although this technical aspect of responsibility would appear to be easily achieved, events can be overlain with complexity and distress. These factors influence the process and outcome for the headteacher. The lack of support a headteacher experiences from the system already delineated is one of the mitigating factors that is overlain on the technical management.

Another societal shift that creates pressure comes from the different roles school staff are expected to perform. The headteacher is expected to guide them and take responsibility for the roles undertaken. The expectations can range from acting as social workers to being a substitute for parents in developing values. Much of this pressure comes from the parents themselves.

Roles of headteachers in the management of grief

The societal changes in the nature of families, parental work environments and the expectation on schools, particularly in creating value bases, have resulted in investing schools with greater responsibilities. That is, headteachers are accountable for their schools' actions and positions on issues other than the academic. This accountability is prominent in the emotive field of grief management. Headteachers encounter disputes with parents about age appropriateness of discussions about death, receive criticism from staff about returning the school 'to normal versus giving students time out', be harassed by the media and be so overwhelmed on a personal basis that they question their competency as professionals.

Given the diverse roles headteachers are now being called upon to perform, having to manage a complex and distressing event in the school community when 'acting' head or in the beginning months of headship is doubly difficult. This can be compounded by a school's history of critical incidents or if the mode of handling the event differs from the previous headteacher.

Fred's death [suicide] *was a fairly rough baptism of fire. The fact that the Year 12 kids were able to go home to their parents and say, 'This new guy is OK', was probably a significant step for me, terrible circumstances from which that is derived, but then the circumstances usually are.*

(Andrew, headteacher for 16 years)

There was a huge response in terms of media and public outcry. That had a big impact on me, because it was so public and because the school was already so badly thought of. That was yet another setback. I really felt called upon to be strong and move beyond the situation that was undermining the school. It's probably the only time in my career where I felt that this is a situation that can make or break me. This was early in my career as a principal. I really was conscious of the fact that nobody was going to manage this unless I did. I could either rise to the occasion or fail.

(Hazel, headteacher for 10 years)

I actually felt I grew up and became more responsible with the first critical incident. I knew then that I was the head. No-one else was there. I had to manage. It was me. I had only been in the job a month or two.

(Emily, headteacher for 3 years)

If I had to rank them, this one is at the top of all the critical incidents in the way I handled it, probably a much more public one than the other ones. It related to what the school had done in the past and so I think it was more a test of leadership.

(Thomas, headteacher for 2 years)

Chapter 3 described the impact of grief on teachers, detailing how their experiences provoke them to question their abilities as competent professionals. So, too, for headteachers, who face conflicts in handling the moral, legal and personal challenges to their beliefs that grief experiences create. If a headteacher is having trouble coping with these challenges, it will become apparent in his or her lack of enjoyment of the job and constant talk about what else is to be done. Instead of processing an incident, it becomes a preoccupation, with a barrage of talk about it, frequently bringing things about the incident back in conversation.

Personal struggles for headteachers

Together with managing grief in the school community, a personal or professional struggle can be experienced by a headteacher due to the events in their private life impinging on their professional life or the loss they themselves experience when a student or a staff member dies. The sense of loss experienced for a student is compounded by the meaning it has for the school leader, who may see themselves as being responsible. The following interchange was recorded by the author. It was one of the few occasions when the re-telling of events overwhelmed the speaker and a request was made during the research interview for the tape-recorder to be turned off:

Brian: *I used to come in here and close the door and wonder what am I doing? The way I found it was . . . outside I had to be relaxed, I had to be confident, I had to be sure, a strength, but sometimes in here, you would almost want to just collapse.*

Louise: *So what did you do to manage?*

Brian: *I didn't, I let it build up. I let it build up, I don't know whether I want to say this at the moment.*

Recording stopped. (The impact of the event was related in confidence.) Recording recommenced.

Brian: *In a way, that is what I do. I think that is what my job is, in any instance it is to look at the kids first, teachers second, senior management next and myself last. That is what the job has got to be.*

Louise: *In this instance, has it had negative consequences?*

Brian: *Yes. A lot of denial. I mean when the doctor told me I laughed, I said, 'Don't be stupid! Me?' She said, 'You better listen to me or it will get worse!'*

Louise: *And how did you come to be at the doctor?*

Brian: *Not sleeping. She asked me questions about my memory and things I was forgetting, lots of other things. That is how she diagnosed it. I have lost an edge. I really have in the way in which I work. You know, it's hard to look at, I mean it was happening . . . It was MY pupils, happening in THIS school. You do take it personally and you take it home with you.*

Paul also experienced a clash of the personal with the professional. Not only had he taught the two students who had died in a tragic accident, but his son was in the same class:

The people around, particularly in a school setting, want to see assurance, calmness, to see that somebody is in control. They look for that. I think that is probably the one thing I have learned. My own son was in that class and Matt and Phil had been on teams I had coached and was a student of mine. I remember that was tough to deal with. Because I got home at night-time and my son had been at school during the day and he had all kinds of questions. Being calm, giving him assurance as a parent. That was doubly demanding.

(Paul, headteacher for 29 years)

For Paul, the emotional strain arose not only from his relationship with his students, but as a parent he also feared losing his own child. For other headteachers, it is their own grief experiences that compound events. There are various sources of this grief: grief as a result of the loss that has occurred or grief from their personal lives – either current experiences or grief of 'the child in the headteacher' triggered by interacting with vulnerable young people.

Headteachers experience a complex interweaving of themselves as a headteacher and themselves as a human being, in their own minds and in the minds of school community members.

> *What do you say, when you walk in to a distraught, absolutely distraught man in front of you? He has the counsellor one side and the chaplain the other. The father looks me in the eyes and says, 'Mr M my boy was so proud of your school and now you've lost him!' I'll never forget those words. I represent the school. That's when it hits! It hits hard. Yes, you do represent the school. It is your school. They do attach it personally to you. You're the man at the top that makes it all happen. I don't quite know what I did say, something about 'I am very sorry I guess'. That was a very difficult day, a very difficult day.*

> (Mike, headteacher for 11 years)

For some headteachers, there is a divide between the personal and the professional, a dichotomy especially in relation to when emotions should be expressed. For others, it has to do with what is kept private and which personal characteristics are part of 'the professional'. That is, an awareness of what is personal and what is professional and what of the personal self is allowed to impact on the professional. It involves the ability to say 'that is nothing to do with the professional', it is kept separate, kept private. A third group believe no distinction needs to be made.

> *I think I probably do put the job first in that situation once the job is over and I have done what I need to do, then I can also allow myself to be emotional. But I will still manage, do what I need to do, but might have tears in my eyes and be upset, but then I would be really emotional when I had some time either with my close friends or my family or by myself.*

> (Jonathon, headteacher for 1 year)

> *The other aspect of leadership is that they understand that you are feeling this as well. I think that if they see you are handling this the same way you would handle a new library, that you haven't got any feelings about it, that is not good.*

> (Lily, headteacher for 5 years)

> *Shelving any emotion of your own. Absolutely, totally putting that on one side. I don't think I really thought about it for at least six months. You couldn't, there was no way. Nobody ever thought about the effect on themselves. Nobody ever, ever said 'I found this very upsetting!' I think we*

all found it very upsetting, but no-one actually said it! It was totally professional.

(Janice, headteacher for 14 years)

I don't think they would think less of me as a headteacher if I cried. I think they would feel sad and would want to support me, but I don't think they would think I was weak. I think the students don't really think of their teachers as whole human beings and so whenever we do anything that shows them we are, it is kind of a surprise to them but rather endearing.

(Hazel, headteacher for 10 years)

I suppose the hard thing is not coming to terms with the fact of what Jim had done [committed suicide], *but really coming to terms with my inability to comfort the father. You expect that as a human being, if another human being is suffering you might be able to ease the pain. But in this first encounter that was exceedingly difficult.*

(Andrew, headteacher for 16 years)

I think grief is very personal and a very private thing. I think a personal reaction in me is that I shrink from public grief, not natural displays of grief, spontaneous displays of grief, but what I sometimes perceive as TOO public displays of grief. I see it is a very personal thing. Its place should be with people that you are close to. But I am well aware many other people are not like that. They feel the need for their grief to be displayed on a more public basis.

(Max, headteacher for 1 year)

Personal adapting

The emotional impact of grief events is often downplayed or ignored by headteachers. Despite intentions to maintain what they perceive as behaviour befitting their role, some headteachers are overwhelmed. Phillip, a headteacher for 12 years, recounts his experience when two students were killed in a road accident in full view of hundreds of other students and many staff:

I found it difficult to suppress my feelings, but kept rising above it and kept going down again. We owe it to the students out there to give them a . . . They are at a much more emotional age than we are . . . We are hardened by experience. [But the impact] *Just never leaves you. It has certainly never left me. And I do think it is of such a significance, well it was to me personally . . . I felt it so deeply, it could have been the finish of me.*

This incident was so stressful that Phillip took sick leave.

When there is a special relationship, there can be a more than the usual 'emotional connection'. This was recognized by Max, who saw memorial services as helping process the loss:

> *He was a charmer and he knew the best way to charm the headteacher. So I would have expected that some time in the future that I would have reacted more emotionally, but that has not happened. We had the two catalysts, the service in school and the service in church. I possibly feel, in retrospect, that any grieving I had to do or sorrow at the loss of someone so young, terrible when that happens, was processed in those events.*
>
> (Max, headteacher for 1 year)

Various strategies are used by headteachers, such as talking and self-reflection. But doubt is expressed as to whether these strategies are always successful.

> *So things are more out in the open now and I think that is good. The more you discuss these things and be open about them, because people do get emotional. The more you are positive, try to look forward and can discuss it with someone who is sympathetic, then that does help. It helps to talk.*
>
> (Geoffrey, headteacher for 15 years)

> *I worry if I could cope with this again. I hope I could, but I sometimes, at 3 o'clock in the morning think, 'Golly they are off on a trip somewhere, if anything happens how are you going to cope?' Then you think, 'Don't be ridiculous, you would do exactly the same, you have the team, you would do it'. I think I probably would, but I think there is a limit.*
>
> (Janice, headteacher for 14 years)

> *I had had my cry, I . . . once we dealt with . . . You get caught up in it, this has to be done, that has to be done and you sit back and talk with your colleagues, you seek advice, I then had been able to go with my two deputies and release a bit. It was important for me just to get angry about one young man dying and another young man being on a life support system, who were smashing kids and it being unfair and things like this and be very angry and be upset.*
>
> (Lucas, headteacher for 2 years)

Some headteachers identified their religious beliefs as a potential source of strength:

> *I have come to this position from a strong personal Christian conviction, a sense of 'it's a vocation', therefore expecting that I would have the qualities*

that are required in these situations. I have spoken to chaplains about this because I have great admiration for them. The comforting thing for me is that they, too, find this difficult. I suspect in these moments of deep grief they, too, find it difficult to find the words to say.

(Andrew, headteacher for 16 years)

Headteachers' management styles

A strong theme in headteachers' accounts of management of critical incidents was decision making that required 'getting a balance' and getting it 'right'. In handling students, there was a need for gentle and sensitive directing of actions and behaviours, balancing their immediate needs with the possible long-term implications for the students and the wider school community.

Debbie was dead, there was nothing I could do about that, she was dead. I mean, we buried her, we mourned her, she was remembered in school. Suddenly flowers started appearing at the door of the classroom and we did not want that, but we did not want to be heartless about it. We have a chapel upstairs, so I said to the kids 'bring them to the chapel, tomorrow morning just before school and put them by the altar and we will share some memories and say a prayer'. It was trying to channel the pupils that way. It was judging the occasion. At what point do you move away from a focus on Debbie and focus on the Year group? It was judging that. Similarly, with staff at what point do you say to the teacher, 'Come on you got some pretty good results last year, what are you going to do this year?'

(Brian, headteacher for 9 years)

I have heard criticisms like 'you didn't know how I felt about it'. I just did not have the time to know exactly how everyone felt. At times there would be criticisms of the effort that is given to the individual versus the group, or vice versa, when you probably either miss some . . . seeing what is happening to an individual, or you are seen to give too much time to an individual. You walk a fine line.

(Bernadette, headteacher for 12 years)

That is also one of the things you have to balance every time, how much is the right response and how much is overdoing it? Oh, that is a HUGE consideration!

(Hazel, headteacher for 10 years)

You make sure you do things as far as you can in the right way with the degree of sensitivity, but you make sure it is done in the right way because this is important.

(Lucas, headteacher for 2 years)

Chapter 5 details how achieving 'normality through resuming routine' is adopted to manage critical incidents. Grief management strategies also involve attending to people, awareness of self as a role model, the use of positive management techniques, focusing on the future and using existing formal and informal systems in the school.

I think the first thing I try and do is to manage the people. Mostly I find that people over-react and there is a lot of talk and drama and gossip. So my first thing is to diffuse that because that is a major thing I find in managing it. Then making sure the appropriate personnel are called. But it is also managing the community. What I find is that if you don't manage the people, the situation gets out of control. It takes more work to put out the fire from the misinformation that is flying around.

(Emily, headteacher for 3 years)

Part of me says, 'did the students milk it?', and a part of me says, 'I don't think so'. We gave them an opportunity to have time out during the next few weeks of school even as far as a month down the track. I guess we acted as a support.

(Joshua, headteacher for 2 years)

The advice we received was that the best thing we could do for the kids and for Matt and Jim and the family is to go on with the routines. They are important. Stay focused on our task here and what we are all about, which is school and learning and move on. What the kids need is a certain amount of structure and routine. As you move further and further away from the centre of the crisis, the kids are impacted less and less and differently. So it is important that those children be kept on their regular routine. But having said that, I remember at the staff meeting in particular, talking to the teachers about allowing . . . If it comes up and they have questions and they want to discuss it, then give them that opportunity. Don't tell them that 'it is not appropriate, we won't be discussing it and now get back to your math'.

(Paul, headteacher for 29 years)

Be really directive. Delegate really effectively with directions. Don't be vague. In a crisis, it is the time to be directive and clear and dot the i's.

(Hazel, headteacher for 10 years)

Recognize that the way you respond is the way that everybody else will follow. I really believe that. That you are critical to the way everybody else will buy into something. If you panic, everyone else will be demoralized and fall apart. Don't be afraid to let other people do things. Recognize your weaknesses. If you are so emotionally fraught, someone else should be speaking to the media. It is not a sign of weakness, it's . . . that's what happens!

(Thomas, headteacher for 2 years)

Positive risk management strategies were used. These involved being able to anticipate impact and perception.

That is something that the administration team are good at. We are good at thinking about what the impact is, what the perception will be, how our staff will receive something, what the students will be receptive to and/or how they will interpret things. One of my assistant principals is very astute in that regard. I am good at anticipating things, seeing things from different points of view. So among us we bring that kind of strength.

(Hazel, headteacher for 10 years)

Management by being prepared, discussing potential events before they actually happen. If A happens, what will the consequence be, just as we teach that to students in terms of their behaviour, know what you are doing!

(Peggy, headteacher for 15 years)

Focus on getting the school back on course in a humanitarian way, not in a careless way. On some days you are going to believe you have reached a crescendo and think, 'Oh we are out of it'. Then the next day you see things and you need to take the atmosphere down a bit and to allow a bit of calm. Lay off a bit when you see tears in the eyes. It is almost like, 'What are you going to do?' should be occupying your energy, more that 'What should I have done?'

(Brian, headteacher for 9 years)

School formal and informal systems have been used as positive risk management strategies. Headteachers whose concept of leadership involves delegation and teamwork indicate the value of using the formal system when there is a critical incident, but also informal communication practices in the school.

Those who wanted to put the pressure on me I called in to explain what I was doing, and I used the informal grapevine, saying 'the boss is handling it right, he wants to work with the family which is appropriate and he wants to be guided by the family and that's the message'.

(Thomas, headteacher for 2 years)

No I have been fortunate and worked with strong colleagues. I have a partnership with my deputy. There are some things I do not do. If something is delegated it is delegated. I am keen in fostering people's professional development and everyone needs training in management. I have always had strong colleagues who know my style well and act in my style. I felt strength in my immediate colleagues but felt very angry about the lack of a proactive forward thinking education authority.

(Peggy, headteacher for 15 years)

Leadership

In the management of grief in their schools, headteachers' philosophies of their roles – that is, their views of themselves as headteachers and visions they have for their school communities – are operationalized. Management of a critical incident can lead to clarification and modification of that philosophy as it is used to guide action and decision making. Headteachers identified links between management and leadership:

You are there to manage and to lead. You are paid to manage whatever walks through that door on a day-to-day basis. But equally, and probably more importantly, part of that job is that you are paid to lead and take that institution forward and if there is any crisis that comes along you have to lead your school out of that and look to the future. I regard that very much as my role. As a headteacher you have to manage but I don't think you can be successful unless you are prepared to lead as well. There is a fine balance between the two.

(Geoffrey, headteacher for 15 years)

When a student who is a 'rogue' or part of a fringe group dies, headteachers identified the need for careful management. There is a need to provide leadership in balancing the school community's espoused values of care for all by acknowledging the death but in a way that does not 'endorse' the individual's behaviour.

I think we have to really try to make sure that any tragedy is considered with care no matter who it is. These were students who had been in trouble with us a lot. The way we responded showed our current kids that they WERE important, they DID matter. I remember one of my assistant principals saying, 'If we undervalue this event it will only be a message to the kids that we don't care because of who they were!'

(Hazel, headteacher for 10 years)

Demonstrating leadership

Leadership requires a vision that frames, explains and justifies actions. A vision that recognizes the 'personal' aspects in management of grief and a personal approach in care for staff:

For me, the key in critical incident management is the follow-up after-care. That to me is where critical incident management really steps in, because it is relating to the mental impact on kids and I say the reluctance is because it is hellishly scary. It is a subjective area, you know to make judgements on whether someone might be struggling with it mentally. I think teachers and definitely administrators, part of you somewhere is a 'tick a box person' and you can't tick the box in relation to how someone is mentally dealing with an issue. I can't get my hands on it but you want to.

(Joshua, headteacher for 2 years)

I mean if you ask them what's my role? I think you need to look people in the eye and see what is going on in their life. I find it extraordinary that people can walk past another human being in a school and be connected to them and not acknowledge them. I mean it is part of being in the community.

(Matt, headteacher for 10 years)

Leadership styles

The style of leadership was seen to be changing:

I think a lot of it does have to do with the kind of human being you are. School councils seem to be choosing different kinds of people than the ones they were choosing a generation ago, so we are gradually seeing the last of the old Heads leaving our schools. By the old guard I guess I am meaning, particularly in boys' schools, the very senior men, who ran very autocratic, authoritarian regimes, because I think they chose to make it so, where they made their individual, arbitrary, non-consultative decisions about all sorts of things without reference to anyone and the deputy just fell into line.

(Andrew, headteacher for 16 years)

There was an emphasis on communication in the school community:

I think the leadership side of it is, in ensuring the confidence of the school community in our decision making, and the way the decision is communicated to the staff, students and the parent community. The amount of time we would put into doing that I think is very critical in leadership.

(Peter, headteacher for 7 years)

Getting to know your school was seen to be important:

I think if we take away, what they call in the jargon, transformational leadership or whether it is strategic leadership or operational leadership, we know all the theory. It isn't, it is actually knowing your school group. It is

conducting an orchestra, that is what it is like. Now, different conductors will conduct the same piece of music in different ways. I think it is letting people be down when they need to be down. To manage it through and bring them up again. It was conducting the school through that. Certainly the year after, right up to the first anniversary, it was very much like that.
(Brian, headteacher for 9 years)

Headteachers have various perceptions of themselves in the management of critical incidents:

I think for me personally, to manage critical incidents, I have to be involved and that requires of me to be definitive in making decisions, but to do so after considered thought and to be seen to be considered in the way in which you make judgements. To be able to demonstrate an empathy with people who are in the situation. You do feel that naturally anyway, but to do it in a way that does not show a lack of control or does not show an over-control.
(Bernadette, headteacher for 12 years)

Leadership from the point of view of mutual respect and what that means with all of its boundaries. I have a style which never allows me to show panic. I stopped panicking externally years ago. Now I panic internally. Sometimes I find now I don't panic till after the event. It is a confidence. I say to colleagues, 'this is what you will project, forget about your personal opinion, this is what we need at this stage'. Respect and lack of external panic are leadership characteristics I utilize. A listening attitude, but being quite clear on the boundaries. The conversation is two ways and I will listen as long as the horn is with the other person and I expect others will listen to me too.
(Peggy, headteacher for 15 years)

The other thing I try to do is be the same. I try to be truthful, open, optimistic and give the sense that 'we are not happy with this but we are managing it and we will get through this'. I try never to appear to be panicking.
(Hazel, headteacher for 10 years)

I hoped that I did not come across as cold. No-one said it. I think that it was being absolutely steadfast and straightforward. People knew exactly what to do and how to do it. It was very instructional and I think that is what they liked.
(Janice, headteacher for 14 years)

I think people look to you, probably above all to be predictable. In other words, that the response that you are making is consistent with the way you behave normally. Now that does not mean that you try to hide your grief or that you are trying to hide your emotions. I think that probably, then, almost more than at any other time, your own integrity, what they have come to understand about you as a person, still has to be there. So being honest with them about how you are feeling is probably more important than maintaining the steely stiff upper lip, non-emotional involvement. So when you are announcing to a group of Year 12s you don't know that one of their class mates has died, you try and keep your voice steady so that you sound 'together', that you try and set an example of 'being together', but being together does not necessarily mean feeling marvellous. So I suppose, then, afterwards, as I moved around among the kids, necessity was that I be genuine about the grief of someone I hardly knew and they knew that. But they would need to see I could be affected by that and also that I could relate to their grief.

(Andrew, headteacher for 16 years)

Listening to where things are at. Hearing what teachers are having to say in terms of their observations or how they are feeling about situations. I think the listening is critical in those situations. Being very observant in terms of what is happening.

(Fred, headteacher for 1 year)

Reflections on the role of leadership in critical incidents

Headteachers had many different perspectives on what constituted leadership in a critical incident. First, standing up for what a school is trying to be as a school and demonstrating support to staff.

The situation where I saw the greatest impact on staff was the shooting because it was so undermining of our work, in building up the reputation of the school before that. The arrest of the teacher was just beyond comprehension. So the staff personalize of course, and then they look for protection and support and understanding. In the shooting case, they needed to know that we were doing something. They were worried about their safety. If somebody can shoot at the front of the school, what next is going to happen? The fear was big. In the situation of the accused teacher, the vulnerability of who is going to be the next teacher to be accused. Who is this student? Who are they going to hit next? A huge fear.

(Hazel, headteacher for 10 years)

Second, showing control to limit the hysteria:

In all of this I saw it as my role, I think it is also a vestige of me as a person, that I explain things very clearly and calmly and how we would deal with it. Whereas if I had not shown control, then I think there could have been some problems, people could have become hysterical.

(Max, headteacher for 1 year)

Third, actions that demonstrate support for staff, students and families:

> *Then I went down to the station to see the kids and to see what was happening there. We just sat around. It was really strange, the kids just wanted to show me. So I went with them and had a walk and a look. For whatever reason they had a deep need to tell me as the teacher or the person responsible for the school.*
>
> (Joshua, headteacher for 2 years)

> *Well all the way through I was telling them they had done everything right, nothing wrong and even if it turns out that the haemorrhage was caused by the machine, the knock the machine gave here, I said you can't stop accidents happening. What we do is we check whether we have done the right things and we have, we have done the right things and there was no neglect, I did not feel there was neglect at all. It was keeping that going and keeping staff informed, step by step.*
>
> (Brian, headteacher for 9 years)

> *What have I got to do to make sure that my boys, my staff, my parents are supported, to do what is right and proper? It is one thing to say you will do what is right and proper, it is another thing to put it into practice.*
>
> (Mike, headteacher for 11 years)

Fourth, being able to coordinate resources:

> *Leadership in terms of I think, being very astute about the kind of resources that are available within . . . and coordinating those kinds of resources, people resources, within the school and outside the school.*
>
> (Fred, headteacher for 1 year)

Finally, being a role model, demonstrating the 'the words' and actions:

> *I had to specifically tell the teachers what to say about the knife. I gave them the words to say and told them they were not to embellish it.*
>
> (Emily, headteacher for 3 years)

> *I had to go to each class and tell them that it was now fact that Matt and Jim had gone and that was really difficult. Even thinking about it now gets me upset* [his voice is shaky], *but I think the teachers appreciated the fact that they did not have to.*
>
> (Paul, headteacher for 29 years)

> *The staff found it very hard, they had to be the Rocks of Gibraltar. They couldn't show any emotion. I myself lost my husband in an accident and I slipped straight back into that mode again. I set that very much as an example. People say we followed your lead. Very practical, calm, no tears, no*

emotion, you are the prop, the girls need you to be like that, you have to be absolutely solid, straight and don't deviate. I was very much like that. The staff very much took their lead from that. There were one or two staff who were going to be emotional and they didn't. They said that. They said they realized you couldn't be. They found that very difficult, because they had to be role models because they were supporting the girls.

(Janice, headteacher for 14 years)

At another level, being able to make the public statements at the appropriate time in the appropriate way. At the assembly I only spoke for two or three minutes about Simon, but a number of staff came and said it was really important to show them how to act. I had to be there in the staff room and say that we would have an assembly.

(Mike, headteacher for 11 years)

Getting support as a headteacher

A lack of understanding of the demands and impact of their role and the beliefs the headteacher and school community members hold about how they should behave and react, all influence help seeking and help receiving. A few systems have employee assistance programmes. For some headteachers, the strong personal support from their team helped them when experiences were overwhelming, such as the suicide of a student. For others, their loss was not recognized and an expression of grief was not allowed (see Chapter 11). Some headteachers advocated and provided examples of the use of more collegial behaviour between headteachers. They also emphasized the importance of support from the system or governing body, but many felt it was lacking:

There is absolutely no structure in place or even talked about whereby people can interact with one another. In fact, our system is really based on people not knowing what the other one is doing. I am in a lucky situation, I have a great district superintendent who said, 'look if there is anything you need, don't hesitate to ask and how are you?'

(Thomas, headteacher for 2 years)

I do think this is quite an isolated job. I think every school is different. Although we have this informal grapevine when it comes to decisions in the school, it is quite isolated, it is a lonely job. I don't think people outside appreciate that nor the LEA realize what it is like day to day, particularly in areas like this.

(Geoffrey, headteacher for 15 years)

Mentors and colleagues were an important source of support for headteachers:

I think there is a certain amount of awareness that there is a problem. I am not sure there are people really offering strategies. I use the [system's] consultant as a sounding board, at the end of the phone or face to face. I came into a role here having been three years in the central office. I knew that larger structure and had confidence in it. Many principals don't share that, they see it as a bit of, this is my kingdom and I won't let the bastards in to find out what's going on! I just feel more connected to that support.

(Doug, headteacher for 5 years)

I think we have become more frank, the job has become harder, more of us I guess are realizing that is it OK to, over a quiet cup of coffee in a meeting, to say to someone, 'Here's what I am facing, what would you do?'

(Andrew, headteacher for 16 years)

Here it is about establishing your own network of people you can ring and say, 'look I need to run this by someone, can you tell me what you would advise me to do here' or 'can you just hear me so that I can just process it with someone?'

(Barney, headteacher for 1 year)

I suppose we either internalize it or we talk to people afterwards, normally our peers or your poor old wife cops it, or husband or somebody cops it sooner or later. But there is no systematic person . . . I often go and talk to the school counsellor about those sorts of things, not in a professional sense, but sit down and talk things through. You find that once you have talked things through, it tends to go away. I am mentor principal for all the new and developing principals in the area. I encourage all principals to have a mentor relationship with somebody else at the same level. That is the sort of networks we build up to be able to handle these things.

(Sean, headteacher for 10 years)

To have helped me I think it would have been more beneficial for me to know that there was some structure in place from above, from the authority that was able to come in, support and advise and create the possibility of counselling for me as a person.

(Ian, acting headteacher for 1 year)

Conclusion

This chapter has documented the first-hand experiences of headteachers in their professional role of managing grief in schools as well as managing the impact of grief on themselves. Although it documents a range of personal and professional challenges, headteachers did see positive outcomes from critical incidents both personally and professionally:

I love my job. I think I am getting better at it, and I feel that I am establishing myself as a principal. It is incidents like this . . . the different highs and lows, I wonder about the long-term impact on me because I am probably one of the younger principals at 45, what's the long-term consequence of being in the job. I want to retire in the same year my wife turns 55, so what are the long-term consequences of this headship?

(Thomas, headteacher for 2 years)

From the research reported here, it is clear that little is being done systematically to delineate the issues headteachers face or to be proactive in putting systems in place, and the policies and practices to support them. Loss in a school community is a defining event for a headteacher:

I spoke briefly [at the funeral]. *I looked down at the sea of faces, every eye was looking up. If there was one good thing that came out of Simon's death, it was an amazing example of the spirit of the school community. It was one of those times in a very sad situation that actually made you very proud to be associated with the school.*

(Mike, headteacher for 11 years)

Implications for practice

- There are many demands on headteachers. They are required to perform diverse roles. They need support in managing critical incidents.
- Headteachers can be personally affected by a critical incident. They can be encouraged to acknowledge the fears and losses without it reflecting on their professional competence. A supportive collegial atmosphere can assist this.
- Headteachers need to consider using the grief management strategies outlined in Chapter 11.
- Leadership can be exercised in a range of ways by various staff members during a critical incident. Members of a school community will expect the headteacher to show leadership through a carefully considered response that takes into account the needs of the school community.

Further reading

Shears, J. (1995). Managing tragedy in a secondary school, in S.C. Smith and S.M. Pennells (eds) *Interventions with Bereaved Children*. London: Jessica Kingsley.

CHAPTER 8

Grief and family/school relationships

Introduction

Although there is concern about the increasing number of social issues that schools are being required to address, 'most families would welcome the school's involvement in a holistic, comprehensive approach to death issues that is in harmony with their values' (Deaton and Berkan 1995: 7). This chapter details a comprehensive approach to school/family relationships by exploring two interwoven themes. These are what families may need to know about grief management in a school context and the understanding school personnel need to develop about family grief to establish supportive interactions. An underlying principle is the importance of maximizing the interchange between groups who become the partners in managing the grief being experienced by school staff members, students and students' families. Within this perspective, an essential tenet is the need to respect the expressed wishes of family members. Two examples exemplify the need for this interweaving. School staff in their ongoing relationships with students 'care' about them, not just in a legalistic sense but in an empathic sense of caring for vulnerable young people. For some this is linked to their care for their own children. Thomas, a headteacher, commented how this struck him: 'I was thinking, this boy is two years older than my own son. How would I be coping if I was the parent?'

The second example relates to how grief can be manifest in schools. Families where someone is dying or has died or where parents have separated are environments where young people may be well behaved, but at school their behaviour can deteriorate. Phillip's mother had been very sick for several years. In the absence of his father, as an 11-year-old he had taken to looking after his mother, getting the doctor or an ambulance if she had a turn and not spending time away from home.

Now a 13-year-old in high school, Phillip's behaviour had deteriorated. The school knew of the circumstances at home but eventually the aggressive behaviour at school required contact with Phillip's mother. She initially did not believe her son's completely different persona at school. In talking the matter through, it became apparent that Phillip's developing maturity had prompted greater awareness of the meaning of the illness and impending death of his mother. He felt he still had to be good at home but could explode at school. These two examples indicate how school and family issues are interrelated and, consequently, need to be examined together.

Changing school and family relationships

In Chapter 1, the changing character of families was described as influencing the role of schools in the lives of children and in shaping society's view about what that role should be. Society demands increasing accountability for social outcomes of schooling. Additionally, the presence of parents and other community members in school governance structures has changed the nature of school management decision making and accountability. The distinction between the role of the family and that of the school in some areas is less clear, particularly as the school may be the one social institution that a family uses for information about parenting and other issues connected with their children. That is, the school is seen as a powerful, authoritative resource for families. One critical incident management team member recounted how the mother of a child who died in violent circumstances called the school for help:

There was a situation where the mother was having difficulty in the home. We got a call that the media was there. She was very distraught, she had the media in the home and could not get them out. She had phoned the school saying she did not know what to do. She had to plan the funeral and couldn't decide on clothing and all the other details. So, we went over there. It was a very intrusive situation with the media. The principal worked with them, moved them out of the home and provided some facts for them. I helped with the mother.

(Sue, critical incident team coordinator for 10 years)

Families now look to schools for resources and practical advice. Yet there is always a dilemma about how far to encroach on family life. In one school where a senior student had committed suicide, the headteacher indicated that it had prompted a change in the way he related to families: 'Where we are worried about a student we now put a bit more pressure on parents to seek outside help than we would have before' (Doug, headteacher for

4 years). The availability, knowledge and experience of school personnel for a family lacking connectedness to their community should not be underestimated by either teachers or grieving parents. Although teachers may need help to strengthen this role and families require encouragement to value the school's expertise, the potential for positive outcomes is great. Mrs Playford explains how she sees the synergy of efforts:

> *At home you teach your child that death is a very sad thing and that to lose a mother or father is very sad. So I think it is the parents who teach the children, but it would be nice if the teachers would throw a bit in there too.*
>
> (Mrs Playford, parent of four children)

When a death occurs, a family may be less skilled in management because fewer deaths are encountered than 50 years ago and because of the decline of extended families, among whom rituals were important learning, information-sharing and relationship-building events. While divorce and the resulting reactions are more common, for some there is still stigma attached and silence surrounding these family changes. One headteacher, Mike, commented that he thought social interactions of parents through school events now performed a relationship-building role: *'Schools are now one of the few institutions that create a sense of belonging. Parents almost use the school to be part of a group rather than just the family'* (Mike, headteacher for 11 years). If a spiritual base is an organizing structure in the school, this assists forming bridges with the family. However, some families find their beliefs in God after the death of a child very difficult to sustain (Silverman 2000).

Supportive role of school for grieving families

Good communication with families, students, parents, siblings and grandparents and the school is essential. The dialogue may be through many staff members, a class teacher, a headteacher or school psychologist. Ian, a deputy head in a primary school, explained the need for this communication:

> *Because the teacher of that pupil has to be the next in line to the parents for actually looking after them because, beyond the parents, we look after the children for the longest time of the day. I think parents would look towards the school and especially the teacher to actually make contact with them to be able to talk to them about the death of their son or daughter and just keep that communication in place, as a benefit for the parents as much for the teacher.*
>
> (Ian, deputy headteacher for 1 year)

Another form of dialogue is information giving, which the school can initiate. Many popular sources of information about children and grief assist in helping parents who may be overcome with the intensity of their child's reactions and the unpredictability of responses (Dyregrov 1991; Mallon 1998). Simple information about the range of ways grief can be manifest affirms for parents the normality of what might appear to them unusual behaviour. Ways to support children are also essential to communicate. With current global television coverage of disasters and other traumatic events, a strong message may be necessary about a supportive process to protect children from the potential negative impact of such coverage. It is important for teachers to inform parents about the need to monitor television watching and use the images as a basis for talking and answering questions.

If there is a critical incident, parents will demand information. This needs to be understood by school personnel as a normal part of the parents' reactions. Parents are trying to understand, not questioning the poor performance of staff. Cognisant of this need at a large high school, a parent information session was convened at the time of a critical incident. Parents and older siblings of injured students were invited to the school a few weeks after the incident to talk about the impact on their families and to enable the school staff to explain further what they had done. Parents and siblings who attended were also given a leaflet about reactions to crisis, so that they might understand better the longer term responses of the young people. Teachers visited the homes of the students who had been injured, thus showing the support of the school. These actions not only provided information, but the parents commented that they hadn't realized until then how caring the school was (Rowling 1994).

Parents have multiple roles as models, nurturers, providers, educators, makers of family rules and managers of family 'climate'. In the management of grief, teachers can help by modelling adult supportive behaviour and by imparting information to parents. This may include information about varying grief reactions that different types of death bring forth, including the death of a sibling from a terminal illness or suicide, the importance of care for survivors – in particular, children – and practical issues such as how the school can be flexible about payment of fees and referral to specialist help. School personnel should also recognise the deep impact the death of a child can have on grandparents (Reed 2000).

Sometimes school personnel are reluctant to contact a family. If a child is misbehaving, it may be decided not to bother a parent who is coping with a dying partner. Or if the loss is the death of a student who has been in constant trouble at the school and interactions with the family have been tense, senior staff may be reluctant to connect with the family. It can, however, be an important healing process for both parties. Hazel recounted her experience:

These were families I did not know, families that the assistant principals had had difficult situations to deal with, probably families that did not think much of us. I remember thinking to myself, 'well in past circumstances I have always phoned those families, I have always offered to visit those families. I need to be doing that'. I did both of those things. I took one of my assistant principals with me on each visit, because they knew the kids better than I did. Also because I knew it would be helpful to my assistant principals to learn how to do that and it would be some sort of healing process for the assistant principal if they had been in a situation of a difficult conversation with the families. Especially in the one case where the girl who died had a grandmother who had lots to do with the school and had felt very badly that her grandchild never did get quite get on track, despite our efforts. It was very good to be able to take him with me and see how grateful the grandmother was and for her to express that to him. It made him feel a lot better I think.

(Hazel, headteacher for 10 years)

Hazel identifies how important it is to have the loss acknowledged by the school. Families often expect this. In another incident in which two students were killed, another seriously injured and a number hospitalized, parents commented that teachers at the hospital didn't talk to the parents and later did not visit the injured students.

Negotiating with families about memorial services and the attendance at them of students is essential. Differing experiences indicate the positive and negative outcomes. A new headteacher experienced criticism from his staff when he did not react as the previous head had:

The year before I arrived they had one of the rogues of the school killed in a car accident. They had a big assembly, they took buses to the funeral, it was bigger than Ben Hur! I think they thought I was cold because I was not prepared to do that unless I worked through the parents.

(Thomas, headteacher for 2 years)

In another instance, the headteacher, because of a previous negative experience, did not negotiate with the family of the dead student and stopped peers going to the house. This was not what the family wanted:

I gave the pupils clear instructions that they should not impinge on the grief of the family. They should not be going to the house, despite how close they were, or how grieved they were. They must give the family time to deal with this themselves. I also sent messages home to parents asking them . . . informing them that they should not take their children out of school to attend the funeral without informing the school. The sister of the boy was in school. She turned up the following day with the message from her

mum – 'thank you for that consideration, that she wanted the children or as many, or anybody to come to the funeral'. This gave me a management problem. So I contacted mum and we discussed this. My wording of the invitation was not as open, I have to be honest, as Mum had anticipated it.
(Max, headteacher for 1 year)

Finding a balance between maintaining order in the school, respecting the wishes of the family and the need for a healing process for peers and the school requires careful consideration of the consequences of various courses of action.

Death of a sibling

For a child, the death of a brother or sister either suddenly or from a long illness can have several short- and long-term consequences. They may be fearful for themselves or others, be anxious about other relationships ending, exhibit impulsive behaviour, be guilty about wasting time or have a sense of urgency to do things now (Davies 1999). A young child may be very confused, expecting the imminent return of a sibling. If there has been a long illness with frequent hospitalizations, less attention may have been given to the surviving child. Conversely, the death of one child may result in hypervigilance on the parents' part. The reaction of older siblings may vary depending on age, a happy or conflictual relationship with their dead sibling, the cause of death and the support available from care-givers. Siblings who have had a fight prior to the death may experience guilt or impending death can bring brothers and sisters closer together. After the death, they may feel guilty, fearing something they said or did caused the death or that they survived and their sibling did not. Or they may feel guilty simply if they have fun. Talking with other siblings in the family can be helpful. Young children having fun is often misunderstood by adults, who think the children are not affected, but it is their way of coping. As seen in Chapter 2, developmental age is important in understanding reactions and thoughts.

Another critical factor is how the child's family responds (Davies 1999). If there are family 'rules' about not talking about a dead sibling, then a child will learn to keep feelings to him or herself, with the possibility of them surfacing unexpectedly, especially in stressful circumstances with peers. Paula recalled the death of her brother two years earlier:

I felt alone, my mother and father never talked and were busy caring for my younger brother. I just felt I had to be extra good. But I was not allowed to help either and felt bad that I was not able to show I loved Toby by caring

for him. In the months after his death, we all on the surface just got on with
our lives, but I didn't – I just got sadder and sadder, but no-one noticed till
my bad end of year report.

(Paula, 15-year-old student)

Bereaved young people may want to return to school immediately, finding the routine and predictability comforting. Their return to school requires planning. Coaching may be necessary from parents or a teacher so that children are able to answer difficult questions or know what to say. It is very difficult to explain 'I had two brothers, but now I have one'. Some young children may be happy for the class to know, enjoying being the centre of attention; others may want to keep it quiet.

Death of a grandparent

Children's and adolescents' reactions to the death of a grandparent can vary depending on how 'connected' they were and the meaning of the relationship. Inter-generational differences may not create the barriers perceived to exist between children and their grandparents. When there is a bond with a grandparent developed through shared activities, through surrogate parenting or where a deep trusting relationship existed, the loss is likely to be intensely felt. The loss deprives a child of an important dimension in their life, but it may be misunderstood or the depth of feeling dismissed by both family members and school personnel. The loss may also have a profound effect on a young person's parents, limiting their parenting ability for a short or extended period of time. For adolescents, the death may have symbolic meaning, especially in their deliberations about life and death.

A dying parent

Many factors influence how young people react to the terminal illness of a parent, including the age of the child or adolescent, the length of the illness and the family dynamics, especially the ability of the surviving parent to adapt to the loss. Where a child comes from a single-parent family, the availability of quality care-givers impacts on the outcome for the child. Young children who have a dying parent may become fearful of losing both parents. Beth recalled how her children, aged 5 and 8, reacted to her spending time at the hospice with her husband:

In the last three weeks of David's life, he was in a hospice. I was able to stay
the night there too. My mother was looking after the children. They came

after school each day to visit, but after a week they became very disobedient and were getting into trouble at school. The hospice social worker suggested that they might be reacting to my absence from home, fearing I was dying too but we were hiding it from them. We sat down as a family and talked about it.

(Beth, mother of 5-year-old and 8-year-old students)

Many dying parents and their partners demonstrate great courage and stoicism, particularly in matters concerning their children's welfare. Mrs Papadopolous explained her philosophy: '*You have to show the kids that you are okay and that life in front of us is there, so they can start pushing themselves towards a goal. If you don't, they are not going to think of the future, are they?*' She was very keen to maintain contact with the school so that staff could understand what was happening in the family and let her know if problems arose. Although her 14-year-old son, George, appeared not to be affected when she was first diagnosed as having cancer, after two years his behaviour changed and he started truanting from school because he was frightened he would come home and find her dead. He did not believe she was telling the truth when she said she was all right. After the school contacted her, George talked with the school psychologist but took a disliking to her, preferring to talk with a male year adviser. He attended school once more but then started having panic attacks, during which his body would stiffen up. Ultimately, he had to be given special leave from school to go to the hospital with her while she had chemotherapy. George's panic attacks stopped, but he still found it difficult concentrating on his schoolwork. Most of the school personnel accepted this and did not put pressure on him, but some teachers persisted in believing he was just trying to get away with doing no work. Mrs Papadopolous wanted the school to be patient with her children, giving them extra help, consideration and a little kindness. She was happy that each of them had at least one adult at the school they felt they could talk with if things were bothering them. But she was still worried about George. She was trying to get him thinking about his future, but he would respond 'I've got plenty of time'.

Family response to a death

If a family has difficulty communicating before a death or divorce, such a negative event will only serve to heighten this. Children in such families feel they are walking on eggshells and may have problems expressing their needs. It is inevitable the relationships in grieving families will change. Stella, a 14-year-old, had shared a bedroom with her

12-year-old sister who was killed in a car accident. After many months, Stella wanted her sister's things moved out so that she could have friends come to stay, but she did not want to make a fuss. This is common when parents are so overwhelmed by their own grief that they are not emotionally able to support their surviving children. In these circumstances, a supportive adult in the school environment can be especially comforting and school personnel may be able to help in the communication with parents.

Lily, a headteacher, recalled the impact of silence in her family and the comfort of a teacher as a 17-year-old:

> *My parents were ones who really didn't want to talk about my boyfriend's death. They had felt the loss themselves, like losing a son. It wasn't talked about at home. It was talked about very little at school. I suppose the domestic science teacher, a person who I will be forever grateful to, at least was prepared to just sit quietly and make sure I did eat something. There was a feeling of 'I don't know what to do to help you but I am here'. I feel that a lot of that grief would have been better dealt with then, forestalling later emotional problems.*

(Lily, headteacher for 5 years)

This death occurred in Lily's last year of high school. Lily went on to relate how, in the impersonal environment of university, her grief got worse and she felt the only way she could regain control of her life was by not eating. It was not until she became anorexic and received bereavement counselling three years after the death, that she began to adjust to her loss. As a headteacher, the experience had greatly influenced the way she organized the school to support grieving young people. She was also sensitive that scenarios in which a young woman was talking about her boyfriend ending their relationship or where he had died, had the potential to trigger an emotional reaction in her. This **resurgence of feelings phenomenon** (see Chapter 12) can be experienced by school staff in interactions around loss.

Silence in grieving families is a natural response, as individuals are protecting themselves and each other from the variety of losses being experienced. The family has to adjust to the changed grouping that is a result of the loss of one member.

As identified earlier in this chapter, the sharing of information about the loss of a family member is not always perceived to be the way ahead. For some families, the need for privacy is paramount, as when a suicide creates family secrets. Schools can cater for the need for privacy, although requirements of duty of care mean they cannot promise confidentiality. Mechanisms for maintaining trust and sharing information on a 'need to know' basis are common strategies, where less detail is available to a classroom teacher than a pastoral care coordinator or year adviser, with the headteacher having more complete information. Students and their families need to be informed of the privacy procedures and need to see the sharing of information as part of the partnership between school and the family. John's mother wanted the school to know about her illness, but John reacted negatively when teachers were singling him out: *'It was not "Hello how are you?", but "How are you feeling?" with a sympathetic tone in their voices'.* As a self-conscious 13-year-old, John felt that by all the teachers knowing, he had lost his privacy and was being treated differently.

Managing conflict with parents

Parents' grief reactions might trigger conflict with the school. Anger at the injustice of the death of a young person might be focused on the headteacher or other personnel seen as responsible if the death has occurred in the school or as part of a school activity. Parents might be experiencing guilt and shame and channel these feelings into something concrete, such as questioning school risk management procedures or threatening litigation. Previous lack of contact or a poor relationship with a family could hamper natural supportive mechanisms, such as when a headteacher has had contact with parents only when there has been a discipline problem with a now deceased child. This negative relationship with the school may limit the family's desire for peer involvement with the funeral or other rituals. Lack of contact by the family with their child's peers might deny the family the opportunity for gaining anecdotal information about their child. In most instances, parents find comfort in contact with friends of their deceased child and schools should try to maintain supportive interactions to allow this dialogue to occur.

School liaison with families

The designation of a member of staff as the family liaison person is important when there is a death or accident at school. This is an important role, not only to offer sympathy on behalf of the school, but to provide support and act as a go-between, explaining what the school will be doing, inquiring about the funeral and ensuring the parents' wishes are considered in all arrangements. Sometimes school personnel need to weigh up the implication of actions for the whole school. Andrew was caught in a difficult situation when a senior student committed suicide:

Another issue that came up that was particularly sensitive was that the parents requested to have the funeral here. All the advice was 'don't do it'. The chaplain talked them through it. We turned the family down about Fred's funeral at the school. I think the way the chaplain handled it was right because not the whole school was affected. We had a guard of honour. A student had to apply to go to the funeral so it was only Fred's particular friends. As far as possible we try to encourage the parents of the kids going to the funeral to be there as well.

(Andrew, headteacher for 6 years)

Subsequently, the school held a memorial service, which the family attended and the student's life was celebrated. Similarly, Thomas, a headteacher, did not want the whole school to attend a funeral as had happened in the past: *'I said, "No, let's be guided by what the parents want". I then went into the personal, "I would not want the whole school there". So we worked it through the year 9 student adviser'.*

Interaction with the family can be difficult. Ian was both acting head of the school and the teacher of a student who was killed one afternoon on the way home. Ian had no experience in expressing sympathy and it took him two months before he could visit the family and return the student's books:

The thing that was hard for me was actually going to the home and approaching the parents about Mark. I was very deeply concerned about the fact that I would say something incorrect, not wrong but incorrect that would upset them even more and that is one thing that I did not want to happen. I did not want to upset them any more than I knew that they must be upset, even two months later. Having NO [Ian's emphasis] experience with dealing with the death of a child before, I just wanted to do the right thing. I did not know WHAT I was going to do nor HOW I was going to approach it to make sure that I did not make the grief even worse.

(Ian, acting headteacher for 1 year)

If a student's sibling or parent has died, school staff who are able to attend funerals can help the student a great deal. Their presence demonstrates care and allows the student to feel secure, knowing that when they return to school they do not have to explain their absence to staff. If a parent has died, a student's return to school may need to be negotiated, both in terms of timing and how much information the student wishes made known.

The need to establish clearly individual actions by staff members as representing a school response was highlighted by Bob:

There was a lot of contact between the school and the families, but we learnt a lesson from that incident. A number of us made contact with various families, but we obviously didn't make it clear enough that we were contact-ing them on behalf of the school. The feedback we got later was that they thought they were being contacted by the individual, rather than the school. There was a criticism that 'The school didn't contact us!' It was a problem amongst the parents, they thought the school had not done enough to sup-port them. Individuals had, but they weren't seeing that if I spoke to them, it wasn't just me it was the school. So we have changed our policy. We have a number of key points that are to be made when we are talking to parents. One of them is 'We are ringing on behalf of the school and you are part of our community and we would like to support you'. We also made it clear that any correspondence goes out on the school letterhead. You can write whatever you like on it, but we were trying to reassure people that the school does care about them.

(Bob, deputy headteacher for 7 years)

Conclusion

The parent community can be supportive but it takes time. You have to build this trusting relationship, build the understanding that we are all on the same side. You can say those mighty words but you have to do it by deed. That takes time. They see how you work and the decisions you make per-taining to their child and their friend's children and they look for consist-ency and fairness. If you can produce that over time, then you are on the right road. But you cannot do that overnight, it takes time.

(Geoffrey, headteacher for 15 years)

The issue of trust is at the heart of the school/family relationship. One headteacher, Matt, identified the trust parents place in the school. He was describing what he saw in the parents' faces when a bus left on an excursion: *'You can see it in the parents' eyes when you are leaving and when you come back. Trust is paramount'* (Matt, headteacher for 10 years).

In proposing a partnership between school personnel and families in the management of grief, school staff will need to consider the limits to the support and services they can provide, given each school's unique circumstances and the availability of outside specialist help. In identify-ing family liaison personnel, there is the possibility of teachers experi-encing vicarious grief where fear of the death of their own children is triggered by interacting with a grieving parent. Care is needed to provide for these support staff. The connectedness within a school community of professionals, young people and family members can instigate natural healing processes. School personnel may underestimate how positively families view staff and the part they can play in the healing.

Implications for parents

- Build upon your children's understandings and adaptive strategies rather than prescribing thoughts and behaviours.
- Talk to your children.
- Be open about how you are feeling but within a child's cognitive and emotional understanding.
- By your behaviour create an environment where your children don't have to appear to be managing.
- Use loss events as opportunities to teach about grief, how to adapt, rituals and remembering.
- Recognize that you may feel helpless in 'making it better' for your child; a comforting hug can convey your caring.
- Be ready to accept great variation in the experience of grief from your children.
- Talk from your heart not your head; respond to the feelings not the words spoken.

Implications for school personnel

- Respect families' wishes, say that the school would want to be involved in rituals and ask 'how would you like us to be involved?'
- As well as offering sympathy to the family of a student, share any personel feelings or anecdotes: 'I enjoyed teaching him science, he was always so curious about animals'; 'Her classmates will miss her willingness to help others with reading'.
- Maximize opportunities for communication with families.

Further reading

Davies, B. (1999) *Shadows in the Sun: The Experiences of Sibling Bereavement in Childhood.* Philadelphia, PA: Bruner/Mazel.

Dyregrov, A. (1991) *Grief in Children: A Handbook for Adults.* London: Jessica Kingsley.

Mallon, B. (1998) *Helping Children Manage Loss: Positive Strategies for Renewal and Growth.* London: Jessica Kingsley.

Reed, M.L. (2000) *Grandparents Cry Twice.* New York: Baywood.

Silverman, P.R. (2000) *Never Too Young to Know: Death in Children's Lives.* New York: Oxford University Press.

Smith, S. and Pennels, M. (1994) *The Forgotten Mourners.* London: Jessica Kingsley.

CHAPTER 9

Partnerships with outside agencies

Introduction

In the management of grief in school communities, there are many service providers – individuals, agencies and voluntary organizations – that a school may enlist to help. These service providers will have their own priorities for the services they provide and how they wish to work. Within the public health framework described in Chapter 1, service provision should focus on two areas: prevention and intervention. Preventive activities involve many of the actions described in previous chapters to support a school community. For many agencies, adopting this proactive approach might be a new way of working, the more familiar process being support of students alone or with family members. Stokes *et al.* (1999) identify the need for services to move in the direction of prevention and intervention, citing examples of agencies now offering comprehensive services that include links with schools. This shift in practice works towards normalizing the experience of bereavement, which helps to reduce the stigma associated with seeing grief interventions as psychiatric interventions.

The conceptualization advocated in this chapter, involving partnerships between schools and these outside service providers, is based on particular beliefs and values and underpinned by collaborative activities. At the heart of this collaborative approach are strategies for shared care for young people between the school, families, care-givers and outside providers. Respect for all in this partnership is essential. In terms of the school–agency relationship, no one group assumes sole responsibility because of perceived expert status, although there are occasions when legal requirements may shift the balance. A collaborative approach assumes that schools, families and outside agencies have needs that they share, and that schools and agencies have time available and financial resources. Capacity-building strategies may be needed to enhance collaborative activities (New South Wales Health Department 2001). Additionally, recognition is needed of hindrances related to individual agendas, varying viewpoints and the adoption of defensive positions. These can affect collaboration (Deaton and Berkan 1995).

Another important conceptualization is the need for a circle of care for school community members, with seamless links between support points and care providers. Support points can be personnel as well as existing school policies and practices, namely the critical incident management plan and pastoral care practices. Instead of isolated points of care acting separately, connections should create a circle of care. This provides for effective referral, where there is an agreed understanding of the actions of each group as well as the limits of parties involved and what constitutes appropriate involvement (Deaton and Berkan 1995). In supporting children, teachers who understand a structure of relationships like this are less likely to feel they are being asked to be psychologists or social workers, something that can deter them from becoming involved. Teachers' care provision would link them with the family, either directly or through an external agency. Similarly, if there is a critical incident in a school, external support people such as religious leaders, bereavement counsellors, police and social workers may initially work with school staff, then support them as they inform students and identify those who need extra care.

The challenges of partnerships

A partnership and support points approach will challenge the beliefs and practices of groups of professionals. Teachers may interact inappropriately with young people (Leaman 1995) or believe that they do not have enough knowledge about grief and so either fail to recognize grieving children or, if identified, refer them to outside service providers. Bereavement service providers, in turn, are knowledgeable about grief, but may not be familiar with working with school personnel and all age groups of children. Additionally, outside personnel may have little information about school procedures, communication mechanisms or policies. They may feel more comfortable working with individual young people than working with the school to create a supportive environment for grief. Their professional beliefs may be such that they may not see the potential of a preventive approach involving teachers, peers and the whole school environment. Nor may they be willing to link with other groups, such as child and adolescent mental health teams or voluntary agencies. That is, a partnership approach requires voluntary and statutory organizations to be prepared to work together. It will inevitably involve clashes of professional beliefs, values and perceptions about whose job it is, who needs the care and where resources should be targeted.

An example of this clash of professional priorities comes from an otherwise excellent resource, *Wise Before the Event* (Yule and Gold 1993). The advice given is: 'Staff needs may be pressing and require attention, but sessions set up by specialists to help staff to help children should not be hijacked to deal with staff members' own difficulties' (Yule and Gold 1993: 42). This quotation labels teachers' needs for support as 'hijacking'. Utilizing a comprehensive approach would acknowledge that, in supporting the staff, the students are also being supported by people they are familiar with and have a connection to. If specialists experience hijacking in sessions they conduct that have the purpose of informing staff how to support young people, then they may need to rethink the basis of their planned approach. If hijacking occurs, then it is indicative that the staff either need help before they can support children or they should not be expected to perform this role if they are so intensely affected. Unfortunately, specialists who conduct these sessions may have fixed views about who needs care and may not understand the dynamics of schools or the roles of teachers.

Outside service providers are most likely to be called upon in times of crisis. Negotiating roles and responsibilities in this context is difficult. A proactive approach to agencies by school communities in the development of their critical incident management plan can see the beginnings of a partnership. If this occurs, in the event of needing outside assistance the school is in a better position to locate quickly the support that meets their needs. Alternatively, service providers, if they have been called to a school as a knee jerk reaction, may have to set an agenda for their interaction with the school, particularly if there is no plan in place for managing a critical incident or no established procedures and practices for supporting grieving students.

It is important to have confidence in people from outside the school. Doug reported how working with an outside agency had changed the way he now saw them:

> *I feel a whole lot more comfortable as a result of the time we have spent together* [with adolescent health service staff] *and our face to face conversations. I would very happily ring them up now and sound them out rather than wait until I had it all worked out or just referring a student.*
>
> (Doug, headteacher for 5 years)

Forming on-going partnerships with schools can maximize the effective use of resources by:

- providing opportunities for proactive actions;
- permitting the tailoring of services and context-specific resources that meet the needs of children and families in a specific local area (Stokes *et al.* 1999); and
- creating links with a broad range of community sources of help (for example, legal and health services and a child's general practitioner), minimizing duplication of activity and maximizing access for children and families to information.

Issues for external service providers

Critical incident management

Johnson (1993) cites an example of a system-based model of management of a critical incident where 17 specially trained school psychologists were gathered to descend upon a school. This was the experience in Janice's school, where 'hordes of people' came to the school to help. This was a school that had no critical incident management plan and was inundated with offers of help. Janice described her experience in detail.

> *They rang and said, 'I'm a trained counsellor, I'll come in and help!' My reaction was 'That's fine!' I wrote all their names down, then I made up a timetable. We didn't say 'No' to anybody. So all these hordes of people* [she laughs], *including grannies who had been counsellors, they all came. We got through it. Looking back on it there wasn't any great gaffe we made, which was lucky. The only criticism was from the girls about the counsellors who came in. They said, 'That lot you had in were hopeless! They were dreadful! There was so and so's parents, surely that was insensitive of you to have them! You realize of course that it was for their* [the counsellors'] *good. It wasn't for our good!'*
>
> (Janice, headteacher for 14 years)

Staff at this school defended their decision to bring in these volunteers, as they felt obliged to accept their offers and did not feel empowered to be selective. They had no plan with names of people or organizations that they might call upon. The experience of Janice's school illustrates a basic premise of this chapter, the need to develop partnerships with schools so that outside helpers are seen as 'consultants to the administration' (Kamins and Lipton 1996: 92). In the United States, a proactive approach is seen as forestalling territorial disputes that can emerge in the context of privatized health care system (Leenaars and Wenckstern 1998). It is essential to liaise with these groups before traumatic events and establish agreements. Divisiveness and further school disruption can be reduced and normality for those uninvolved maintained. At the emotionally charged beginning of a critical incident, negotiating relationships between an outside critical incident management team and the headteacher is not an ideal strategy. Nevertheless, this is what some schools are required to do if they have not developed their own management plan.

Being proactive allows external support personnel to assist school personnel to feel in control. When a critical incident occurs, the conditions for optimal functioning of outside helpers will vary, but there are some basic principles that need to underpin this cooperation:

- There should be a rapport between school personnel and outside helpers so that there is a shared understanding of what a school requires.
- School personnel should recognize the technical expertise outside helpers offer.
- If the school has a school counsellor or educational psychologist, those from the outside providing counselling need to work alongside or under the guidance of that person. This has three functions. It provides:
  (1) the outside helpers with access to inside knowledge about the school;
  (2) a mechanism for the provision of on-going support, after the team have left; and
  (3) critical friends to support the school counsellor or educational psychologist, headteacher and critical incident management team.

Outside helpers find it challenging when school personnel are insistent on pursuing a course of action that the external group's experience indicates may not result in the best outcome. One psychologist from a local education authority said:

The most frustrating times have been when we have principals [headteachers] *who are going to do it their way and they are not going to listen. I try and present it that 'you are in the situation and you are closest to the students and the family and sometimes in those situations it is very difficult to deal with the grief, because you are so close to the situations, so you can allow us to support you with that'.*
(Clarissa, educational psychologist for 10 years)

One headteacher recognized the expertise possessed by outside helpers. He reported sitting in on a counselling session the outside team conducted with his students:

I sat in on and off during the day and was so impressed with the skill base of the people. Questions I would never have thought to ask, feelings, visualizing, things I would never have thought to do. As a head of a secondary school, I would have thought ticks and crosses, we've done that and that and then move on. It was a much more fluid, user-friendly experience that I got to listen to.

(Joshua, headteacher for 2 years)

The contribution of external help was recognized by another school. It was in the grip of a threatened meningococcal epidemic and could not get information about a student from the hospital. Local health workers were able to act as intermediaries and obtain the necessary information. Also, when there are large numbers of migrant families in the school community, religious groups can not only be supportive but can also help with communication.

Mike recognized the positive contribution of outside help: *'Something told me I had to have this assembly but I didn't know what I was going to say and how I was going to say it!' They* [the outside team] *were very helpful in talking around what needed to be said and done in that hour'* (Mike, headteacher for 11 years). In some schools, proactive management of a critical incident is in its infancy. Hence David was prompted to say:

I continually give thanks that we had already had contact with those outside services. At that time in our school structure, there were no counsellors, no-one trained to be aware of what to do in those situations. I had to work out a proforma to contact parents. I think with any incident you have to seek outside advice, specialist advice, very quickly. The strength of the community then is how you use that advice to deal with the situation as it occurs.

(David, headteacher for 7 years)

One headteacher, Brian, was personally affected by an incident:

It was about 6 weeks after. It just hit me. Had we not had Amsden Social Services behind us from the word go, I am not sure we would have come through as we did. There are some very strong people in Amsden. They certainly helped me, helped my staff and the counsellors certainly helped the pupils.

(Brian, headteacher for 9 years)

In a situation that involved possible criminal charges, Kevin was aware of the need for specialist advice from the police: *'If it was a stabbing or an attack of some form or other, then the advice is not to contaminate evidence and not to contaminate witness evidence'* (Kevin, year coordinator for 12 years).

But not all support personnel work effectively with schools. One school encountered police making judgemental statements:

One of the coppers who was interviewed by the local media said, 'Oh the kids of that school just run all over the place everywhere at lunch time', which was straight nonsense. The copper just had to make one of the broad brush sweeping statements that police do on occasions and it got reported in the local media and that was anything but helpful.

(Sean, headteacher for 10 years)

Failure of the police to inform a school about the murder of one of the students had repercussions for teachers and students in another school:

I believe the police handled it exceptionally poorly. I heard it on the news coming to school. I drove up into this road and saw kids streaming home crying. The boss had not been told. The police and the parents of the girl, where the murdered girl was staying, came to school to tell the headteacher what had happened. The headteacher was so shaken, he was a very Christian man, he nearly collapsed. It was just not handled well, no-one knew. The girl was sort of on the edge, if you can understand what I mean. They were all a bad group of girls. We had terrible gang warfare for a week after.

(Trish, teacher for 15 years)

Dissatisfaction with outside help can occur when agencies are not sensitive to the 'cry for help' from school personnel. For example, a headteacher of a primary school had constantly been seeking help from a government-funded health agency because of the increasingly bizarre behaviour of an 11-year-old girl. Even when she had what was later identified as a schizophrenic episode in front of the whole class, the agency did not respond. The headteacher was left locked in her office with the student not knowing what to do. The student was bashing her head against the wall, sitting in a fetal position moaning and rocking, and trying to stab herself with sharp objects. The headteacher felt helpless but feared the student might increase the harm she was inflicting on herself if she went home. It took more than two hours of this behaviour before the student was calm enough to be taken to hospital. The student was released the next day and arrived at school with no contact having been made by anyone at the hospital with anyone in the school. For the headteacher, this was a critical incident. She was not only deeply affected by the event but felt ignored and let down by the lack of support. After pressurizing the hospital staff for information, it was found that the age of the pupil had prevented them acknowledging the symptoms the headteacher reported as being linked to schizophrenia.

Debriefing

External service providers are likely to be caught up in decision making about debriefing. It is important that there is no harm done either by interventions that undermine the natural healing processes (Wraith 2000) or by treating people as casualties needing to be fixed by professionals. As noted in Chapter 5, there is controversy about who will benefit from debriefing. In arriving at a decision about debriefing, the distinction between grief and trauma is important. Outside agencies called in to assist, whose work involves palliative care, may not be aware of the differences. Trauma involves excessive fear and panic, feelings of vulnerability and an exaggerated 'startle response' to unexpected sights and sounds. The re-experiencing of the events is not just of re-occurring thoughts, but intrusive and distressing thoughts, images and nightmares that relive the terror, helplessness and horror of the events. These memories can interfere with grief reactions as the traumatized individual stays in the event, not integrating it into their life (Klicker 2000). Traumatized school personnel and students are the ones likely to benefit most from debriefing.

Developmentally appropriate debriefing

Stallard (2000) identifies some important differences in the reactions of primary school age children and adolescents to traumatic events. The younger age group have the cognitive capacity that enables them to talk about or re-enact different endings for traumatic events. Surprisingly, while adolescents have a greater cognitive ability to construe meanings, their fear of exposure of thoughts and feelings with peers may silence them in a group environment.

Debriefers from outside agencies may not tailor their approach to the children's needs, but follow a prescriptive formula. Such protocols may meet the debriefers' needs for a standardized approach, but not the needs of the children and their context. For this reason, formal debriefing as a language-based intervention that follows particular specifications may not be in the best interests of children (Wraith 2000). The following requirements detailed by Wraith (2000) are needed by participants for the group technique of debriefing: cognitive, communication and social skills; self-awareness and self-regulation; and a capacity for confidentiality. If children have not reached this developmental level, they could be drawn in a group to disclose something that is not in their best interests and to identify with the experience of their peers to an extent that is harmful. Those providing psychological first aid need to be:

• known and trusted by the children;
• know each child developmentally and functionally;

- have an understanding of child development, childhood trauma reactions, childhood psychopathology and family and group processes; and
- be trained in childhood debriefing processes (Wraith 2000: 209).

Several general aims of debriefing can be pursued with young people if it is considered relevant as a concept, process and technique. These aims are not unlike the requirements for adults and include the opportunity for emotional relief, to have their feelings validated and receive reassurances about the appropriateness of their responses, and to receive developmentally appropriate information to help understand the responses and learn some management strategies for now and in the future (Wraith 2000: 199). Issues that also need to be considered within a developmental context are the involvement of parents and the peer group. As young people age, there is likely to be a shift from parents to peers, although there could be complicating factors, such as children who are in boarding schools and who rarely see their parents. Other issues that would need to be considered are: readiness for the experience of debriefing; level of engagement in the process; self-disclosure and confidentiality issues; limits to available coping skills; the possibility of re-traumatization and the need for trained debriefing leaders (Wraith 2000: 200). Potential harm can occur when personnel with limited skills carry out debriefing. This harm could be a result of re-traumatizing and then not being able to manage this within the group.

In school communities, the word 'debriefing' has many connotations. One interpretation was made by Fred, a former member of an outside team that went in to help schools:

For the staff in the school, they come back together and look at what they have learned, what they have been through . . . a kind of building together and sharing. I think that is a real healing process. I think in the earlier times when we went in and kind of dealt with the situation, we did not necessarily do stress debriefing of all the staff afterwards, and I now think that is critical.

(Fred, headteacher and educational psychologist for 8 years)

Sean, a veteran of many critical incidents, was in favour of debriefing:

I don't see a problem with debriefing. I just think the more you talk about things, the more chance you have to keep it in perspective. You don't recycle it in your brain 1000 times until it becomes something that it should not become. That is why I see debriefing and talking it through as being a necessary step in management.

(Sean, headteacher for 10 years)

Jill referred to putting on her critical incident hat. She believed that *'The critical incident management team have to then come together after the incident and debrief and come out of role and respond personally to the incident'* (Jill, deputy headteacher for 3 years).

For many school community members, debriefing is talking about the events and reviewing what was done – that is, operational debriefing. This can include a feeling component, but the teaching/information aspect in a formal debriefing protocol is not part of their interpretation of debriefing. The main achievement of these actions is the creation of a sense of control and regaining the normality so critical to school functioning.

Particular characteristics of schools may influence the impact of a critical incident on staff and create the need for psychological interventions by outside services:

- A school community is characterized by emotional connection and ongoing relationships between staff and also between staff and students.
- The adults in this environment have direct responsibility for the lives of a vulnerable group.
- Staff in general are 'untrained' compared with emergency services workers. A culture of 'mental preparation' as a natural part of the training of teachers does not exist.
- Schools are workplaces for individuals whose 'art' is planning, thinking, telling and discussing. Controversy about management is likely as people think issues through in terms of critical incidents.
- Most of those being supported will be children. This creates high stress (Robinson and Mitchell 1993) and can intensify negative reactions, such as: a great sense of injustice when youngsters are killed or injured; and a sense of personal vulnerability, as school staff are likely to be parents, thus heightening their identification with a dead or injured child's parents.

For some emergency services, such as the police and firefighters, critical incident stress debriefing is mandatory but not compulsory. That is, the organization puts systems in place and legitimizes the time for processing and review. This may be an appropriate model for education systems and individual schools to follow. Schools have found it helpful to talk with others who have experienced the same or similar situations. The outcome of these 'shared experiences' has been to leave those affected feeling generally less isolated and more reassured.

Debriefing is just one form of intervention in schools. An informed school critical incident management team will be able to work with outside helpers to identify the circle of care that needs to be implemented when a critical incident occurs.

Provision of support, individual and group

As well as working to support schools, bereavement service organizations offer grief counselling and group support programmes for young people. For young people, these groups help normalize grief, provide support, allow the opportunity to vent feelings – especially anger – and offer suggestions for grief management. Some children and adolescents will find organized support groups extremely beneficial, but they may not match the needs of all. This may be a result of the 'model of grief' being used in the support group. For example, it may be based on getting children to express their feelings, work through tasks of mourning (Worden 1991) or talk about common grief experiences. Much bereavement counselling has as its basis talking therapy. This is one form that provision of care can take. But environments are needed that validate the various ways of expressing grief. For young males these include diversion and reflection (Martin and Doka 2000), processing by action rather than verbally expressing feeling; and by thinking it through rather than talking.

Leaman (1995) recounted counselling experiences of young people who felt that counsellors try to hijack the emotions of their clients and take them somewhere they do not want to go. This could be due to a lack of understanding of different styles of grieving, the counsellor operating on a model of phases or stages, trying to fit the young person into their model. Martin and Doka (2000) provide some useful guidance about developing more open approaches:

1 Be intentional. As a counsellor, understand the aim of the strategy being used and seek to assist cognitive processing or trigger the venting of feelings.
2 Choose strategies the client is comfortable with. Some individuals are comfortable with creative arts approaches, such as music. Others may prefer storytelling. People who are uncomfortable verbally expressing themselves, however, may not gain from this approach. A negative experience may even stop them from seeking help in the future.
3 Build on strengths. Identifying strategies used successfully in the past may assist an individual in managing their grief.

On-line support

Technology is providing increased opportunities for support that is readily accessible during the various cycles of grief. Young people in particular like to use the Internet because it is interactive and anonymous. For service providers, it is a cost-effective way to convey information. Traumatic events that might have been local events now have national and international impact. But instantaneous support is available on the

Internet. The need for a moderator to facilitate sessions is necessary when strong emotions are expressed or where numbness inhibits dialogue (Gary and Remolino 2000). There are benefits and limitations of on-line support groups. The benefits include: increased access, reducing the sense of loneliness and isolation; the opportunity to participate in a specialized group by age, nature of loss or gender; and the recognition through the experience of the universality of loss, enabling people to have a sense of a shared experience. The limitations include: breaches of anonymity, putting an individual at personal risk of cyberstalking or having their privacy invaded; differing stages of group development and differences in patterns of grief; perpetuation of hoaxes; limited feedback, especially the decreased intimacy from a lack of face-to-face feedback; and accountability that relates to legal, ethical and professional issues (Gary and Remolino 2000). With many of these issues unresolved and like other strategies for support, on-line groups may not be appropriate for everyone.

Change and capacity building

For change in the work practices and structures of organizations outside the school environment to be developed and sustained, clarity is required of purposes and outcomes, quality practice needs to be identified and self-monitoring mechanisms need to be adopted. Bereavement service organizations should aim to:

- normalize grief in the community by providing access to resources;
- reduce the stigma associated with grief support and counselling; and
- increase the capacity of others to acknowledge grief and, if necessary, to provide appropriate referral (Stokes *et al.* 1999).

New measures will be needed that match objectives for the development of links and partnerships. Guidance for this comes from recent activity in the health promotion field, where the emphasis on capacity building of individuals and organizations to promote health has resulted in the development of indicators. Capacity building involves strategies for organizational development, workforce development and resource allocation (New South Wales Health Department 2001). These are supported by leadership and partnerships. Capacity building occurs within particular contexts. Strategies and approaches need to take account of these contexts at all times. Indicators to help identify effective partnerships include time set aside to review and renegotiate planned actions, monitoring of how resources are used and the gathering of further resources (Hawe *et al.* 2000).

These are examples of capacity building across agencies, but there are others within service provider agencies themselves. For example, workforce development will be required to allow adjustment to changed roles within organizations. Further details about this are provided in Chapter 12. While the variety of action areas and approaches needed to build capacity may appear overwhelming to schools or agencies, thinking in this comprehensive way allows action areas to be identified that are within the human and financial resources of the organization.

Capacity building can enhance quality practice. The accomplishment of quality practice can be demonstrated through effective monitoring procedures of service provision by charitable or non-government organizations. This provides accountability mechanisms and enhances these organizations' capacity to demonstrate efficiency in financial expenditure from statutory sources as well as local and national fundraising.

Conclusion

Changes in professional practice, school organization and service providers' ways of working have been themes in this chapter. Change is threatening for people and organizations; however, if it is acknowledged and managed, it can have positive outcomes. The professional roles of teachers are strengthened when they act to create school environments that provide grief support, not only for students and their families but also for their colleagues, and to enhance the educational outcomes for students. Learning and working will be improved and connectedness to a school that cares will be augmented. This acknowledges the importance of schools as social institutions in families' lives. Improvements in broader mental health outcomes can also be achieved.

Service providers, particularly those focused on bereavement care, often struggle to provide a broad range of services with diminishing resources. Forming partnerships with schools and links with other organizations and agencies can increase efficiency and effectiveness. This will involve capacity building and a reorientation of organizational goals and work roles for some agency workers from working in one-to-one counselling or support groups to being facilitators and providing technical advice to enhance the practice of others.

Implications for practice

- A proactive approach by schools in developing partnerships with external agencies can help ensure appropriate support is accessed by the school in the event of a critical incident.

- Additional support provided by an external agency can help the school manage a critical incident.
- Careful thought needs to be given to the place of critical incident debriefing within the management of a critical incident. A plan that makes appropriate debriefing available but not compulsory could be considered.
- Capacity building within and between organizations will assist the formation of effective partnerships.

Further reading

Deaton, R.L. and Berkan, W.A. (1995) *Planning and Managing Death Issues in the Schools*. Westport, CT: Greenwood Press.

Klicker, R.L. (2000) *A Student Dies, a School Mourns*. Philadelphia, PA: Taylor & Francis.

New South Wales Health Department (2001) *A Framework for Building the Capacity to Improve Health*. Sydney: New South Wales Health Department (available at http://www.health.nsw.gov.au).

Stokes, J., Pennington, J., Monroe, B., Papadatou, D. and Relf, M. (1999) Developing services for bereaved children: a discussion of the theoretical and practical issues involved, *Mortality*, 4(3): 291–307.

Smith, S. and Pennels, M. (eds) (1995) *Interventions with Bereaved Children*. London: Jessica Kingsley.

Wraith, R. (2000) Children and debriefing: theory, interventions and outcomes, in B. Raphael and J.P Wilson (eds) *Psychological Debriefing: Theory, Practice and Evidence*. New York: Cambridge University Press.

CHAPTER 10

Special cases

Introduction

One of the features of the loss and grief field has been the in-depth exploration of a number of specific issues around children, adolescents and grief. In this text, the focus is the school community. This chapter concentrates on specific issues and populations in the school context. These issues are categorized as 'special cases', not with the intent of stigmatizing or separating them out, but of acknowledging their place in a school's management of grief. The coverage here provides an introduction to the major challenges to be faced in addressing these issues. For those requiring more detailed information, see the 'Further reading' section at the end of this chapter.

Issues

Suicide

The suicide of a student or staff member is greatly feared by the school community. Statistically, the likelihood of a suicide in a school is small compared with other causes of death. However, the stigma, suddenness and emotionality surrounding the event, and in the case of young people the potential for suicide attempts by peers, requires that the event be even more carefully managed than other loss and grief issues. The suicide can be inexplicable and it challenges perceptions of the natural order of things. For those schools who have no critical incident management plan as described in Chapter 5, the experience of the school community can be particularly stressful: 'The school collectively becomes the suicide survivor and, in that respect, is subject to all the emotions of any individual survivor: guilt, anger, anxiety and denial' (Petersen and Straub 1992: 148). Planning to manage a critical incident does not indicate the expectation of a suicide; rather, it demonstrates responsible risk management practice.

Controversy

One of the difficulties for school personnel is the perceived lack of agreement between mental health professionals about suicide prevention. Hazell and King (1996) provide an informative account of the arguments for and against prevention programmes. Although this debate has resulted in many schools choosing to do nothing, other teachers argue: *'Not teaching about it is a poor option. If it does come on the agenda and you don't address it, you are failing the students. It's us that have the hang-ups, they want to discuss it'* (Jay, teacher for 9 years). In the absence of clear evidence about effectiveness of suicide awareness programmes in preventing suicide, recommendations have been made that, 'due to the suggestibility factor in relation to suicide, teachers are advised not to undertake specific "suicide awareness" units or to prescribe suicide as a central topic or sole focus for research or creative projects' (Cahill 2000: 12). Conversely, 'because schools have an enormous amount of consistent and direct contact with a large population of adolescents, they are a strategic setting for the implementation of suicide prevention programs' (Klicker 2000: 93). Part of the controversy about suicide prevention and intervention arises from the parameters of the research methods used to assess the impact of programmes, for example: suicide ideation and students' anxiety; the lack of clarity about terminology such as suicide prevention and intervention; and the nature and form of interventions (Hazell and King 1996). There is a big difference between a three-hour educational session conducted by someone outside the school system and a session that is part of an ongoing programme conducted by a staff member or team of school personnel familiar to the students (Schmitt and Ellman 1991). The latter comprehensive approach is recommended (Centers for Disease Control 1992; Kalafat and Elias 1995; Hazell and King 1996).

A range of activities has been funded in Australia under the National Youth Suicide Prevention Strategy (Commonwealth Department of Health and Family Services 1997). One of these is guidelines for the management of suicide in schools, *Educating for Life* (Cahill 2000). This document places suicide prevention/intervention and postvention in a mental health promotion framework. Within this framework, the recommendation for secondary schools is that all staff should be aware that any instance or thought of self-harm requires serious attention: 'Staff should pass on concerns about worrying behaviour or disclosure of suicidal thoughts' (Cahill 2000: 40). Many myths exist, however, about suicide in particular. Thus, if students talk about it, they are not serious, and suicide attempts are only strategies to get attention. It is important that training dispels these myths. Suicide has a complex aetiology, so it is essential that staff receive training not only about signs and symptoms but also about depression and the different ways it can manifest itself in students. This recommendation arises because a consistently identified risk factor for suicide and suicide attempts is depression (Klicker 2000).

Risk and contributing factors

In addition to depression and other mental illnesses, other risk factors include a previous suicide attempt, substance abuse, family conflict or dislocation, cultural conflict and sexual orientation. There are also precipitating factors, such as grief about a loss of significance to the young person, legal problems, abuse and interpersonal problems. In a school environment, factors that might be particularly noticeable are: being the target of bullying; low grades or the perception of academic failure; feeling overshadowed by siblings; high expectations of self or others; perceived inability to form and maintain relationships; and feeling disconnected from the school community. In isolation, no one of these is a great predictor of suicide.

Suicide prevention

Based on current evidence, a comprehensive approach is recommended (Petersen and Straub 1992; Kalafat and Elias 1995; Cahill 2000; Klicker 2000). Such a recommendation is differently interpreted by having either a comprehensive mental health promotion perspective (Cahill 2000) or a comprehensive ecological approach with a student, staff and community focus (Kalafat and Elias 1995; Klicker 2000). The former may not necessarily include direct reference to suicide in classroom work with students, but would involve awareness raising with staff about suicide.

'Training educators to help and understand children who are grieving is an effective suicide prevention tool' (Petersen and Straub 1992: 145). Unfortunately, many educators hold beliefs that discount the worries and concerns of young people. Janine commented on her colleagues '*It* [suicide] *is an area which is almost completely ignored, because most people can't handle it. Many do not believe prevention programs are necessary, the "they'll get over it attitude"*' (Janine, teacher for 14 years). While encouraging peers to seek help for a depressed friend has been a focus for many interventions, too much responsibility should not be placed on them. Boundaries need to be established. These will specify that a good friend listens, cares and supports his or her peers, but does not provide counselling in circumstances where self-harm, depression or suicide are possible. In the school environment, discussing problems needs to be seen as acceptable behaviour and a sign of effective problem solving rather than a weakness. Principles that can underpin classroom discussions include:

- If you are worried about a friend, tell an adult; take all threats and warnings seriously.
- If you suspect a friend is really down, ask how they are feeling and, if they don't want to talk, pass on your concern to someone who could intervene.
- Don't make a promise to keep suicidal plans or thoughts a secret.
- If you made a promise before knowing that it involved a suicide threat, it is important to break it if someone's life is at risk.
- Suicide is not a good choice. Young people should be helped to find a better solution. Most people who commit suicide send hints beforehand.
- When someone threatens suicide, they often have a mental health problem that is treatable (Rowling 2000).

Effective referral processes of which all staff are aware are also good suicide prevention practice. Threats may be disguised by students in art, drama and English. Teachers need to be alert to these subtle hints and pass on their concerns. For teachers, this process involves developing an awareness of their responsibility to refer students. They should not take on a counselling role but be able to distinguish between being supportive and caring and counselling. If the risk is high, then immediate steps are necessary to ensure the safety of the student. The school needs to inform parents or care-givers and consult with them about referral and management. A school–community partnership, with external support services experienced and trained to work with young people at risk, is desirable. This can provide information immediately and strategies for shared care can also be developed (Cahill 2000). Respecting the student's right to privacy means that information is shared on a 'need to know' basis. Planning for reintegration into the school after a suicide attempt is essential. This should include discussions with peers, if the attempt is known to them, and assistance from all teachers to help complete assignments. The student should be consulted about what information can be shared, especially if there are rumours, and there should be ongoing contact with the family and external agency.

Postvention

When a suicide occurs in a school, it can shake the community's core beliefs about whether they are living up to their publicized aim of being caring. Teachers and families experience a sense of powerlessness, which results in judging and blaming the victim. Doug, a headteacher, related the impact of a suicide on his staff:

The staff were a bit angry and frustrated, asking 'why can't the experts tell us what we should do [nervous laugh] *and why a student still commits suicide when you believe you are doing all the right things?' We did a lot of soul searching as we believe that one of the great strengths of this school is our pastoral care and counselling systems.*

(Doug, headteacher for 2 years)

A death by suicide requires carefully considered management. This may be different from the management of other deaths, especially in relation to peers who may be at risk because of previous vulnerabilities or suicide pacts. Identifying all these young people is essential. The possibility of a strong emotional response requires care in announcing the death. The staff need to be the first to be informed. They should be given time to react and also be given information about the management of students' reactions, the school's plan and what to say to students. The stigma associated with suicide might result in the means of death not being disclosed; however, withholding the truth is not advisable as it fuels rumours. Age-appropriate explanations of suicide should be given (Klicker 2000). The students close to the deceased student should be told privately away from others.

Practices that might occur for other deaths may need to be modified. One headteacher reported that he had to take on the role of supporting the parents and staff, a role he would normally have a deputy headteacher take on. Funerals at the school have the potential to exacerbate problems. Andrew recounted his actions:

In my previous experience we had very difficult funerals. This had arisen from episodes where the student had virtually been extolled. So that any kid that was a bit twitchy sitting in the congregation might well think, 'hey this kid is famous! I am never going to get recognition like this'. At one particular funeral at another school, almost a heroic response developed. We developed a tacit policy amongst ourselves that as far as possible we would discourage funerals at the school. About 6 weeks later we had a memorial service here. It was an open ceremony. Virtually everybody in year 12 came, plus a lot of the families. We did not have all the padding of a funeral, just a celebration of the boy's achievements.

(Andrew, headteacher for 16 years)

As detailed in Chapter 5, a critical incident management plan is essential, with a special section about suicide management.

In recent years, there has been intense media coverage of suicides in schools due to violence. These have most often been associated with the use of guns, by students or intruders. Although death from violence in schools is not new, what is different is the number of multiple victims (Anderson *et al.* 2001). But schools are not powerless. Effective preventive measures that are comprehensive can limit outbreaks of violence. These measures require staff and parents to be informed and alert to changes in young people's behaviour and to have well-established intervention mechanisms. The approach to suicide adopted here acknowledges the need to have suicide management strategies in place for those students who attempt suicide and those who do commit suicide. It also emphasizes the need to strengthen known protective factors, including connectedness to school, increasing help seeking and help receiving skills, creating a sense of optimism, resilience and maximizing the social support within a school community. Sometimes it is in the year or two after leaving school that young people commit suicide. Schools can extend their protective role by assuming a sense of a 'continuing community'. This involves conducting exit interviews with students to ensure that they are aware of support agencies, and leaving the door open for the students to return for help or to return and provide guidance and mentorship to existing students.

Different population groups

Children from distinct populations or subgroups, such as refugees, immigrants, ethnic minorities and indigenous peoples, can be at risk of negative consequences of loss experiences. Although culture may add to their risk, the greater exposure to losses may be a more important influence on outcome than their cultural background. School personnel developing an encyclopaedic knowledge about different cultures will not improve their sensitivity to the ways and symbolism of another group or to the logic and forms of etiquette required. Rather, a willingness to observe, listen, ask and learn from the people themselves is required. Sensitivity also involves being 'outward looking' or separating personal feelings from the behaviour of others.

Young people of non-English-speaking backgrounds

For children and their families of non-English-speaking backgrounds, two issues relating to loss and grief need to be understood and incorporated into the actions of the school community. The first is understanding the losses experienced during transition to life in a different country, and the second is the acknowledgement of the cultural practices and beliefs around death, dying and trauma. Schools have a vital role to play here, because they have the capacity to provide a trusting and trusted environment to which people can belong. This is in contrast to the possible negative environment experienced in the wider community. The losses encountered are mediated by: an ability to speak the language of the country of residence; experience of war and trauma or other forms of organized violence prior to migration; whether their destination was chosen or allocated; and the available support networks (Hurley 2001). The specific losses experienced include: family and friends; sense of security; loss of name, identity, confidence and objects of sentimental value; and loss of a way of life such as beliefs, traditions, celebrations and an integrated community. Many of these losses continue while new ones emerge. For example, when older adolescents feel caught between two cultures, they may grieve for not being able to fulfil their parents' expectations, but at the same time not identify completely with young people from an English-speaking background (Hurley 2001).

The initial response of a child who eventually settles in a school environment can be intense sorrow for all they have lost. Schools can assist students' adjustment to these losses by providing structure and predictability in the classroom and links and connectedness with families. Having lost trust in systems of authority, the school might be the one social organization in which students develop trust. In some circumstances, family members can develop post-traumatic stress disorder with profound consequences for the children (Hurley 2001).

Indigenous youth

In this section, Indigenous young people from Australia are used to exemplify some of the issues faced by these groups. The persistent and ongoing nature of the losses experienced by the Indigenous community in this country deserves special attention. This coverage is not meant to suggest that all Indigenous peoples' losses are the same, only that there can be some similarities that influence their **meaning making** of their loss experiences.

The grief of Indigenous people in Australia shows significant differences from that of other groups, most notably: continuing grief related to the dispossession of land; removal of children from families; and loss of community and cultural heritage. A cycle of ongoing grief can be experienced by families, including the incarceration of family members and frequent suicides, particularly of young men. Indigenous losses are also a result of premature mortality, ongoing racism, socio-economic disadvantage and transgenerational loss.

It is important to recognize that Indigenous communities have structures for supporting grieving members. These structures include tribal elders, consultative councils and long-established practices of care and support that may vary with location and language groups. Some groups have cultural practices that are the antithesis of an Anglo-Celtic view of grief, including the practice of not mentioning a dead person's name. Loss and grief is a collective experience as well as an individual one for many Indigenous Australian young people (Hurley 2001). It is essential, therefore, for a school to ensure that commemorations in the school are culturally appropriate for the diversity of school community members. Indigenous young people may be uncomfortable about approaching school personnel for several reasons, including: a lack of personal knowledge of a staff member; being embarrassed, 'counselling' being an unfamiliar experience; not wanting to talk to a non-Indigenous person, as this may be considered taboo or be related to a perceived lack of confidentiality; and distrust in services and fear of decisions being made for them (Hurley 2001).

Other special cases that need to be addressed by school communities include young people who have been abused, young people of same-sex orientation and those with disabilities. Culturally sensitive care needs to be provided to diverse school community groups. This can be achieved through acknowledging rituals of particular groups. The psychological effects of rituals include the physical closeness of others provided by practices that place the loss in the realm of life experiences. These promote a sense of continuity in the community and of the place of the individual within that community. The positive outcomes for individuals are a sense of emotional release and feelings of inner strength (Rosenblatt 2000). These processes and outcomes can also occur for rituals that school communities perform when one of their members dies or rituals for reclaiming the school after violence has disturbed the sense of safety.

Chronically ill and dying children

School has a vital role in supporting chronically ill and dying children, adolescents and their siblings. It is essential for the class teachers of a child with a life-threatening illness as well as other school staff to maximize opportunities for the child's participation in as many aspects of school life as possible. An empathic class teacher can develop an individual learning plan for an ill student. This not only keeps them up to date academically, but helps maintain a sense of the future and a sense that life goes on as normal and they are like everyone else. The school can provide an opportunity for the child to maintain an identity as a student rather than as a chronically ill or dying child.

The child's illness and return to school can be a chance for the class teacher to increase other students' awareness and skills in being empathic and tolerant, especially in preparing for the return of a child to class.

This will help to avoid teasing and isolation. The return to school needs to be carefully thought through. The appointment of a staff member to coordinate this is advised, particularly in the secondary school environment (New South Wales Cancer Council 2000). The coordinator may need to remind teachers of the need to make modifications to assignments or sporting activities and create unobtrusive support in the classroom and playground. If the student dies, class members should be included in funerals if both the dead child's parents and the class members' parents agree. Negotiating these issues is described in Chapter 8. Class members should also be supported in identifying a means of appropriately memorializing their peer's presence in the school.

Parents may need support in telling siblings about their brother's or sister's illness. Teachers are in an ideal position to 'coach' the parents in the provision of age-appropriate information. Schools need to be involved in a case conference with parents and the child's doctor and nurses. They need to have continuing access to these people, especially if the child is attending school in between treatments. Specific information that teachers require includes details of the illness, its treatment, any limitations to the student's activities, how much the student knows about the illness and what the family would like the child's peers to know. The class teacher of a child with a life-threatening illness may need the support of other staff members.

For the adolescent with a life-threatening illness, their concurrent developmental changes in physical appearance, relationships with peers and sexual identity compound the losses experienced as a result of the illness. Feeling and being different may dispose them to withdraw from social interaction, especially if their physical condition precludes them from engaging in the normal activities that occupy peers. Healthy peers grappling with discovering who they are can draw back from a classmate with a life-threatening illness. Knowledge of the illness and its consequences can help these young people interact with their sick peer.

Siblings of chronically ill children often suffer greatly but also report positive outcomes as a result of their experience (Davies 1999). The most common reactions include feeling forgotten, overloaded, frightened for their parents and their ill sibling, angry and jealous of their sibling but then guilty for feeling this way. They can experience anticipatory grief, changes in living arrangements, no holidays, limited opportunities for participating in sport and an ultimate change in identity as everyone asks about their ill sibling, without being interested in their own activities. The comprehensive analysis of sibling bereavement by Davies (1999) conceptualizes the variables that affect bereavement as individual, situational and environmental. From a school perspective, what is important to note is that a bereaved sibling may perform poorly at school, either behaviourally or academically, often as a result of their inability to concentrate. However, this is not always the case, as some may overachieve as a way of escaping their grief (Davies 1999).

Special schools

Schools that accommodate chronically ill children, such as those with cerebral palsy, cystic fibrosis and muscular dystrophy, face grief management issues that are different from those faced by mainstream schools. Both health and education professionals, as well as a number of aides, will have close daily contact with the students. In an education setting, the health professionals are often not under the direction of the head-teacher. This can create tensions around procedures and information sharing, especially when a child is dying. Additionally, the presence in the schools of aides who develop close relationships with the students as they care for their physical needs, can be a difficult management issue when a child dies. With limited training, they may not have developed the ability to set boundaries on their relationships with the students and as a result care for them as a parent would. The young people are likely to use the opportunity of the close contact with the aides to ask questions about their sickness and dying. The aides are therefore at special risk when a child dies.

Calling in an outside team to help support children and staff when a child dies may not result in the best outcome. Jonathon reported what happened in his school: '*School counsellors who had never been in a special school came here to support people. They were coping with their own reactions and were uncomfortable because of the student's disabilities*' (Jonathon, head-teacher for 1 year). The staff made the decision and wrote it in their critical incident management plan that in future they did not want outside help; if people did come, they wanted them to be familiar and comfortable in the environment.

Conclusion

This chapter does not present the definitive answers to the issues raised. Rather, it offers insights and suggestions for action. It is necessary to challenge assumptions, to develop new ways of conceiving the issues that can be translated into innovative practice. Some of the young people identified in this chapter will have ongoing feelings of loss as they perceive they will always be seen as 'different' (Hurley 2001). An underlying tenet for actions is the need to consult individuals and the specific communities concerned when managing these special cases of loss and grief. Major aims for school communities should be to engender feelings of safety and trust and to reduce stigma.

Implications for practice

- Ensure staff receive information and professional development about disabilities, same-sex attraction, suicide and working with young people from diverse cultural backgrounds.
- Engender feelings of respect for individuals and their families, their values, beliefs, cultural practices and lifestyle choices. Verbal statements and ongoing practices should reflect this respect.
- Strategies for reducing stigma need to be addressed through the school curriculum.
- A variety of approaches need to be provided for students to be acknowledged and affirmed and to become connected to the school and its values, and to the staff.
- Ensure that the privacy of staff, students and their families is maximized even if events cannot allow confidentiality.
- Create safe places in the school environment where students can feel free from harassment.
- Maintain working partnerships with outside agencies.
- The concepts of help seeking, help giving and help receiving should be familiar in the school environment.
- Ensure that the commemoration of the death of a student by suicide is appropriate.

Further reading

Bluebond-Langner, M. (1996) *In the Shadow of Illness: Parents and Siblings of the Chronically Ill*. Princeton, NJ: Princeton University Press.

Cahill, H. (ed.) (2000) *Educating for Life: A Guide for School-based Responses to Preventing Self-harm and Suicide*. Canberra: Commonwealth Department of Health and Aged Care (available at http://www.curriculum.edu.au/mindmatters).

Davies, B. (1999) *Shadows in the Sun: The Experiences of Sibling Bereavement in Childhood*. Philadelphia, PA: Bruner/Mazel

Hazell, P. and King, R. (1996) Arguments for and against teaching suicide prevention in schools, *Australian and New Zealand Journal of Psychiatry*, 30: 633–42.

Klicker, R.L. (2000) *A Student Dies, a School Mourns*. Philadelphia, PA: Taylor & Francis.

Ministerial Council for Education, Employment, Training and Youth Affairs (2000) *Report of MCEETYA Taskforce on Indigneous Education* (available at http://www.curriculum.edu.au/mceetya).

New South Wales Cancer Council (2000) *Kids and Cancer: A Handbook for Teachers*. Sydney: New South Wales Cancer Council (available at http://www.nswcc.org.au).

Petersen, S. and Straub, R.L. (1992) *School Crisis Survival Guide: Management Techniques and Materials for Counsellors and Administrators*. West Nyack, NY: Centre for Applied Research in Education.

Smith, C.C. and Pennells, M. (eds) (1995) *Interventions with Bereaved Children.* London: Jessica Kingsley

Tatz, C. (1999) *Aboriginal Suicide is Different: Aboriginal Youth Suicide in NSW, ACT and New Zealand: Towards a Model of Explanation and Alleviation* (available at http://www.aic.gov.au/crc/oldreports/tatz/index.html).

CHAPTER 11

Disenfranchised grief in schools

Introduction

School community members and school systems are at various stages of recognizing and responding to grief (Rowling and Holland 2000). As described in Chapter 7, many headteachers believe they have to suppress their natural reactions in response to a loss in their school. Pfefferbaum and colleagues (1999) maintain that parents and teachers underestimate the extent of young people's reactions to traumatic events. Reporting a study of youth after the Oklahoma City bombing, they encourage 'active inquiry about symptoms of trauma and grief' (p. 1378), because these can be hidden by young people. Research has also identified hidden grief in teachers (Rowling 1995).

The concept of hidden grief or **disenfranchised grief** has been defined as 'the grief that persons experience when they incur a loss that is not or cannot be openly acknowledged, publicly mourned, or socially supported' (Doka 1989: 4). Disenfranchised grief may arise because the relationship is not recognized, the loss is not acknowledged or society does not give the person that role (Doka 1989) because of the circumstances of the death and the way individuals grieve (Doka 2002). In a school community, there are a number of sources of disenfranchised grief – self, others and the social world of the school. Although there are similarities between schools, each school is unique, with its own history, relationships, rules and procedures that often reflect particular cultural and religious values, beliefs and normative behaviour. This is especially important because meanings about loss experiences (cognitive representations of reality) come from the culture and others' expectations mediated through an individual's internal resources and life experience (Rowling 2002). As a cognitive activity, this meaning making can be altered. Throughout this book, instances of grief being hidden in schools because it is unrecognized, unaccepted, or there is stigma attached, have been identified. This has the potential to create problems for these individuals and the school itself.

This chapter describes school community members' experiences of disenfranchised grief and the sources of that disenfranchisement, which are self, others and the wider community. In doing so, the experience of students, teachers, parents and headteachers will be interwoven with the sources through individual personal appraisals, gender and role expectations, social norms and values. As already identified in Chapter 6, school communities can create the conditions that limit these sources of disenfranchisement by recognizing and acknowledging grief. The chapter concludes by examining the 'cost' of enfranchisement, in terms of the number and type of changes school communities might have to make.

Sources of disenfranchised grief

Self

While recognition and disenfranchisement of grief occurs in a social context, there is also an intrapersonal process in operation. Kauffman (1989) believed that the sources which are inside the person or those that are societal tend to blur and may be difficult to differentiate. Individuals can disenfranchise their own grief. They may not recognize or acknowledge their grief and so restrict their behaviour, even though that behaviour may be socially determined. That is, their lack of acknowledgement of a reaction or recognition of this loss comes from within. The feeling behind this is shame (Kauffman 1989). Individuals impose restrictions on themselves regardless of whether society does. The influencing factor is not the true values and beliefs of others but the imagined views of others. The grief is not just silent, unnoticed or forgotten grief, but grief where there is 'a more or less active process of disavowal, renunciation, and rejection' (Corr 1998–99: 6). Disenfranchised grief that has an intrapersonal source can be a result of: shame about one's emotions; shame about the exposure of self that might occur in grieving; shame about the hallucinatory experiences grieving individuals may have; and the memories of restrictions grieving rules placed on the expression of previous losses (Kauffman 1989). Intrapersonal sources of disenfranchisement result in dislocation from support in a community, depriving an individual of the opportunity for natural healing.

Other people

In the context of the social world of a school, the beliefs and values of the headteacher, teachers, students and parents can shape the behaviours of all these people. This is done through grieving rules, relationships, gender and role expectations and acceptance (or non-acceptance) of the impact of loss experiences. A school establishes grieving rules, which are sets of norms created by the school community. For example, the school can specify the amount of leave staff are allowed for deaths, for whose deaths leave can be taken and how much allowance is made for grieving students. The formal policies might be determined by a centralized authority, but schools do introduce 'informal' practices (Rowling 1995). Grieving rules may also exist between families and the school, for example when a school has an unwritten policy never to hold memorial services for students.

In school communities, relationships may involve strong attachments between students, students and staff and between colleagues in a particular school or with staff in neighbouring schools. These attachments may not be recognized. Events that occur within schools may not be identified as losses for the school community, for example when a teacher is accused of abusing a student. Teachers' expected professional behaviour, such as the need to control emotions yet be a caring person, to be in control of a situation and to provide 'duty of care', is established in a particular school environment. This, however, may also limit their grieving. Particular expectations of behaviour established by a governing body, parent association or a predecessor might codify the behaviour of a new headteacher in a school. That is, a school community can create role expectations surrounding the concept of professional behaviour of a teacher and the headteacher. Similarly, where a school has a counsellor or educational psychologist on staff, the expectation may be that this person should be able to manage their emotions irrespective of the circumstances.

For all members of the school, grieving patterns may be prescribed by gender. If a staff member dies, judgements made about appropriate behaviour in an all boys' school by a principally male staff may be different from those made in a co-educational school by an executive composed of a mix of males and females. While being male or female does not result in a specific grief reaction (Martin and Doka 2000), in an all boys' school there may be particular rules about 'being a man'.

As already identified in Chapter 2, the parents of children in early primary school may fail to recognize the loss their children experience. They believe that their children's cognitive development precludes them from experiencing the loss.

Wider society

Beliefs, personal meanings, grieving rules and a supportive context are key elements for sanctioning loss and grief in a school community. But wider societal influences can be the source of disenfranchisement. A centralized educational system may not have in place policies that support school-based decision making about leave or allocation of resources to manage grief when there is a critical incident. A change in beliefs about the purposes of schools, the professional roles of the teachers and educational policies and structures is necessary for educational systems if they are to be supportive.

For many losses, stigma is attached, affecting the way a school may react, what individuals believe and how they respond. One 17-year-old, Dennis, was adapting to the increasingly unusual public behaviour of his father, who at 45 had developed a mental illness. Only one of the teachers in the school knew about this because of Dennis's fear about the stigma associated with mental illness. The teacher encouraged Dennis to participate in a grief support group in the school. In the group, the young man was able to realize that he was not only mourning the loss of his dreams of a future with his father, but also that he was not allowing himself support (disenfranchising himself) by not telling friends.

A death due to a drug overdose can be silenced in a school community for fear of public disapproval. Chapter 1 identified the increase in societal disapproval of school performance through public criticism and censuring. This fear of censure may limit acknowledgement of the loss. The disenfranchisement can be fuelled by the media, especially if the death involved a perceived lack of duty of care. For example, Andrew reported:

> With Bruce's death, there were more serious duty of care implications because one of the papers got hold of the idea that it was a punishment run, that he had been made to go on this early morning run because he had been naughty. And that was not helpful. The idiot reporter said he was there as a boarder 20 years ago and punishment runs were a regular part of the programme, all this sort of . . . pretty unhealthy for a while. The media are pretty cruel to boarding schools anyway.
>
> (Andrew, headteacher for 16 years)

Disenfranchised grief of school community members

Headteachers

The beliefs that headteachers hold about their role influences how they behave. A professional role such as that of a headteacher is personally as well as socially constructed. Within the role of the professional there is a personal self. These can be intertwined so that they are indistinguishable or a headteacher can act to keep them separate or make decisions about what is kept private, and which personal characteristics are part of 'the professional'. It is during the experience of loss in a school that difficulties can arise. Professional expectations disallow the personal response and force individuals to believe they must 'rise above' their natural inclinations. This is exemplified by a headteacher who described what he thought his role required:

> *We are better able to rise above it . . . You have a responsibility to your students and staff to provide leadership, the right leadership . . . a moral obligation to provide leadership and understanding and to sympathetically guide the student into accepting the reality of life.*
>
> (Roy, headteacher for 38 years)

This headteacher's unsteady words were recorded seven years after an incident when two students were murdered. But Roy did not 'rise above' the incident. At the time of being interviewed, he did not reveal the impact of the event on himself. But a number of years later his reaction was related to the author when she was interviewing another headteacher about the impact of critical incidents. The second headteacher related what happened. (The headteacher did not name his colleague, only the school. I did not indicate I knew of the event or that I had interviewed the headteacher who had kept his reaction hidden. Similarly, no-one else in the school had revealed the outcome. It had become a school secret.) Roy had locked himself in his office and and left his deputy to manage the crisis. He subsequently took leave.

Actions taken in a school community that recognize and acknowledge grief do not always have the support of all staff, who have their own beliefs about the expression of grief. But where criticism arises, senior staff can verbalize the reasons for particular actions as part of the supportive school environment that is being created, thereby publicly stating the school's grieving rules and its commitment to enfranchisement.

Hazel believed that male and female executive staff had different ways of reacting to grief:

> *Women pay more attention to the communication needed and the feelings, the emotional response of people, valuing the strengths that men and women bring to the situations including crises. A recent comment from a male principal shows this. He said, 'I don't expect to cry. I pride myself in not crying, I was not going to cry'. But I think he meant he did cry.*
>
> (Hazel, headteacher for 10 years)

Beliefs about the expected grief reactions and behaviours of males compared to females are particularly relevant for the adults in a school community. These beliefs tend to focus on particular adaptive strategies that are seen to be more characteristic of either males or females. They have as their basis a difference in expression of thoughts and emotions, more specifically the beliefs and the existence of verbal expression compared to no verbal expression (Martin and Doka 2000). A less disenfranchising approach would be to look at verbal expression of feelings compared with other forms of emotional expression.

Teachers

Like headteachers, the perceptions teachers have of themselves in the role of a teacher influence beliefs, experiences and actions around grief in schools. The accounts that teachers provide of their roles demonstrate that they have strong personal involvement and attachment to students. These relationships, however, are not recognized when it comes to the death of a student, especially in traumatic circumstances (Rowling 1995). The emotional response to the empty desk in the classroom may not be recognized as a personal loss.

A traumatic incident can threaten a teacher's professional role. Staff are responsible for students, so if a student is injured a teacher's competence is open to question. There is also the potential for criticism through the media and the parent body. Teachers may recognize that the reputation of the school is threatened even at risk of being lost, but more importantly the grief reaction may not be identified. It can be dismissed as 'being angry'. Teachers' concepts of professional competence involving 'having the answers' and being able to control events that happen to students could be threatened by a critical incident. The problem is that grief is a phenomenon for which there may be no answers to questions such as 'why did this student have to die so tragically?' Teachers may not recognize that not having answers when their students die poses a threat to beliefs in their professional ability. Their unrecognized loss is evident in their thinking: 'if I can't help or protect young people, am I a competent teacher?'

Teachers' views about being competent in their role also relate to being in control of their emotional state. When discussing their professional role, teachers cite being in 'personal control' as a determining factor of their behaviour. 'Breaking down' in front of the students concerns them. Teachers infer that this behaviour conveys a message to students that weakens a teacher's professional standing. Shame over one's emotions is a major source of intrapsychic disenfranchisement (Kauffman 1989). A source of this shame is one's perceived inability to perform one's role.

Between teachers there can be prescribed patterns of appropriate behaviour for the expression of grief. Joy, a classroom teacher, was angry with her head of faculty because he did not behave as she believed he should:

'Look Joy', he said to me, 'I nearly . . . I nearly broke down and cried, but I didn't, I did the right thing, I didn't cry'. So for him, not crying was very important, but for us that he did cry was very important. I expressed my anger to my colleague and said I was disappointed in his reaction.

(Joy, teacher for 9 years)

If individuals through their beliefs or school communities through their structures, policies and practices have been disenfranchising grievers, there will be some staff and students whose earlier grief has been unacknowledged and unsanctioned. Kauffman describes the impact of this as:

The effects of the earlier sanctions and the consequent unprocessed grief have become part of one's present grief reaction; the experience of the new grief is disenfranchised by intrapsychic forces brought into being by the earlier disenfranchisement, despite the existence of any significant social disenfranchisement in the present situation.

(Kauffman 1989: 28)

This resurgence of feelings phenomenon means that schools with teachers (and students) who experienced past traumatic events that they managed by ignoring and suppressing will bring these experiences to subsequent incidents. This was the case in Kair High School in New South Wales, Australia. When I carried out my research there from 1991 to 1993, there was frequent referral to an incident five years earlier, indicating the existence of 'the memory of unsanctioned grief' for staff. It was also found by a debriefing team to be a confounding factor in the debriefing of a critical incident that occurred in 1993. The school management of the later incident did acknowledge the earlier event and its potential to revive memories, and support was offered. The incident was socially sanctioned. Some teachers could not utilize the support, but it did help others. The sanctioning of possible grief reactions to the crisis provided an opportunity 'for a grief that was disenfranchised many years earlier to emerge and be acknowledged' (Kauffman 1989: 29).

A teacher's specified role is not equated with that of emergency service personnel, nurses or social workers (Newburn 1993). Yet teachers perform a role similar to those of other helping professionals. They are helpers and carers and provide support for young people for whom they have a responsibility and with whom they have a personal connection. Teachers' grief can be socially sanctioned through statements in critical incident management plans and the practices of managers. For teachers, it is their professional role in a particular social context that is a major source of their disenfranchised grief (Rowling 1995). In such circumstances, the meaning of the events is created in part within the school community. It follows, therefore, that the school community, not just a teacher's family and friends, needs to provide support.

Students

As mentioned earlier in this chapter, age can be a source of disenfranchised grief for younger children. But for adolescents, the sources are more numerous. Friendships, both same-sex and opposite-sex, are of great importance and create complex meanings in young people's lives. They help establish identity and provide companionship, emotional support and opportunities for intimacy (Oltjenbruns 1996). The deaths of friends and broken friendships result in multiple losses, the impact of which adults often minimize or fail to even recognize (Rowling 2002). Broken love relationships are dismissed as minor hiccups. This may increase students' withdrawal in school, not only affecting their academic progress but limiting the help and support they receive from others. If a peer dies, the absence of knowing how to behave (grieving rules) may cause a young person to resort to conformity to peers' expectations.

Gender can be a significant disenfranchising issue for young males in schools. Uncertain about their sexual identities they can be greatly influenced by the confining behaviours of perceived masculine grieving patterns. Thomas, a headteacher, was concerned about the absence of male counsellors who could present a pattern of grieving for the boys in the school: *'There were a lot of boys involved* [in the counselling], *but all the counsellors were female. I thought where's the role models for these boys, that say, it is okay to grieve, that it is okay to cry?'* (Thomas, headteacher for 2 years). The pattern Thomas wanted, while not traditional for young males, was still a prescribed one that may not have been useful for some males or some females. Codes of acceptable male behaviour may be absorbed from a young age. Mrs Brown marvelled at how closely her son's behaviour matched his father's:

> *The thing I found interesting is that my husband covered his emotions up enormously and my eldest son* [aged 10] *is doing the same, yet he never saw the extent his father covered his emotions given the difficult job he had. My son is exactly the same* [as his father] *and if I sit down and want to talk about how I feel, he tells me to be quiet. He can't even cope with me wanting to express how I feel.*

Environments are needed that validate the various ways of expressing grief. Options for young males that need to be sanctioned include diversion and reflection, processing by action rather than verbally expressing feeling, and by thinking an event through rather than talking (Martin and Doka 2000; Doka and Martin 2002). Sanctioning can also occur by providing information on grief reactions and adaptive strategies. It is important young people are encouraged to see that there are different forms of grief and that their options are increased by examining what is working for them in terms of adaptive strategies and, when they get blocked, knowing the alternatives (Rowling 2002).

A loss experience that singles out a young person and results in behaviour that is atypical or that indicates difference is concealed by the adolescent. There is fear that the peer group will not sanction unique or unpleasant feelings or characteristics that do not conform to the individual's required role in the group. In this process, the adolescent denies themselves support. Oltjenbruns (1996) has characterized this as 'double jeopardy', the experience of loss and the felt need to hide this. The source of shame is the perceived views of their peers. As well as covering up grief experiences for fear of being different or being seen to be different, young people may maintain secrets because of feelings of inadequacy and a lack of control in loss situations (Raphael 1985). The major developmental tasks of seeking independence and being 'in control' of your life are another source of disenfranchised grief.

An additional source of disenfranchised grief is the perception of teachers and parents that it is not the school's role to support young people because in doing so there is an intrusion on the privacy of families or on perceived parental roles. Yet if the grief is connected with school members, it is the school environment where the meaning is created.

To influence the sources of disenfranchisement in young people, the different pathways that young people follow as they learn to cope must be recognized. In addressing intrapsychic disenfranchisement, exploring an adolescent's sense of their own biography about loss may assist in identifying their unique construction of experiences, including an exploration of lost fantasies as well as lost realities. Peer relationships exemplify the paradox of disenfranchised grief. Because peers do the disenfranchising, work needs to take place with peers as well as the griever. This paradox supports the value of discussion groups to young people, which include information giving (psychoeducation) about the normality of grief and the 'hearing of others' stories' (Rowling 2002). Adolescents who are taught about loss and grief may understand better a peer's experience and limit the sanctions covertly applied.

School counsellors and educational psychologists

For teachers, one source of their disenfranchised grief is that they are placed in a caring role. They are personally affected in that role if a critical incident occurs in a school and one of their students dies, but their loss is not recognized. For school counsellors or educational psychologists, there is a different source of disenfranchisement. It resides in their expectations of themselves as professionals who have a specific responsibility to help everyone. So they, too, see the importance of being in control of their emotional state because, if they are not, how can they help others? They perceive that because others see them as dealing with emotional issues all the time, they can handle every situation. The loss they experience is of their core professional beliefs. A similar phenomenon has been identified in social workers involved in disaster management: 'There were widespread and deeply held views about the need for social workers to remain "strong" to "be able to cope" or, rather more extremely, to avoid being seen as "someone who is likely to crack up"' (Newburn 1993: 135).

Sarah described how she reacted to a critical incident in a school to which she had been newly appointed. She, like many headteachers interviewed by the author, saw this incident as her test. Although she became exhausted, she did not recognize it and her family did not acknowledge it:

The level of exhaustion I felt I had not expected. I was just absolutely exhausted each day. When I went home my eyes hurt, it hurt to close my eyes. I don't know why, perhaps it was the stress you feel in your head. I was irritable with everyone else outside the school, particularly anyone who did not give me the time I needed to sit and be left alone. I told my husband and he said 'It was just an accident!' I couldn't cope with having to justify what I had done. One of the things that concerned me was that there was no recognition from the school system of what I had been through. Police have the day off or there are other practices. Not so for schools. Many of us were quite sick in the weeks after that event.

(Sarah, school counsellor for 14 years)

Enfranchisement of grief in school communities

When adopting a comprehensive approach, major hurdles exist to the enfranchisement of grief in schools. Some teachers need to change their conception of their role, from a teacher of a subject to a teacher of children and young people. Also, there needs to be public acknowledgement by school officials of their relationships and their losses. Generally, this is not the case for teachers. In a school that sanctions grief, practices are developed on the assumption that grief is normal but that it can trigger problems that can be solved. The sanctioning of grief by the educational system has occurred. For example, in the state of New South

Wales in Australia, it is now mandatory for all government schools to have a policy to manage critical incidents (Rowling and Holland 2000). As Joy recounted, this has prompted schools to act, *'because of the requirement to formulate a critical incident policy, schools/Principals have facilitated inservicing [sic] of staff in this area by their school counsellors. This might not otherwise have happened'* (Joy, teacher for 9 years).

School environments need to establish grieving 'norms' for their community. If referral to counselling is the main strategy of a plan, vulnerable adolescents may see the strategy as adults and peers perceiving that they are not adapting. This can result in personal withdrawal, which forestalls community mechanisms for healing. Special relationships between those who have suffered the same stressful experience may provide a 'therapeutic community' effect. This allows people to talk through what has happened, share feelings and support one another in several ways, which may help recovery (Weismuth, cited in World Health Organization 1992; Nader 1996). School communities can create the environment for this 'therapeutic community' effect (Rowling 1999).

For many teachers, the norms of the world of work disenfranchise them because emotional reactions are 'discounted, discouraged and disallowed' (Stein and Winokuer 1989: 92). The recommendation for workplaces is that training is provided for managers so they can understand grieving employees, and for employees to enable them to understand their own grief.

Conclusion

The research reported here suggests that schools need to create environments that are supportive of grief experienced by members of school communities. These caring environments acknowledge the experiences of young people and support them individually and in groups. These schools do not deny the impact of these events, but have plans in place to manage them as well as support staff. From a mental health perspective, this proactive approach demonstrates a caring ethos for individuals and establishes caring as normative behaviour – with its potential positive mental health outcome of 'connectedness to school'. Whilst the changes required may be large in some school communities, the benefits of enfranchising grief have important educational outcomes.

Implications for practice

- It is important to recognize all types of losses that can occur in a school community.

- Actions taken by schools during a critical incident need to recognize and acknowledge grief.
- Headteachers and other executive staff, as well as school counsellors and educational psychologists, can ensure the school community is supported by sanctioning the provision of professional development, information exchange and counselling.
- Students experiencing a loss can benefit from individual attention and grief support groups. It is equally important to teach all students about loss and grief so they can understand better their peers' loss experiences.
- Environments need to be created that validate the various ways of expressing grief.
- Staff in schools can feel pressured to remain 'in control' when a critical incident occurs. Strategies need to be in existence to enable the losses that staff experience to be identified and acknowledged and thus minimize the impact of disenfranchised grief on teachers.

Further reading

Corr, C. (1998–99) Enhancing the concept of disenfranchised grief, *Omega: Journal of Death and Dying*, 38(1): 1–20.

Doka, K.J. (ed.) (1989) *Disenfranchised Grief: Recognizing Hidden Sorrow*. Lexington, MA: Lexington Books.

Doka, K.J. (ed.) (2002) *Disenfranchised Grief: New Directions, Challenges and Strategies for Practice*. Champaign, IL: Research Press.

Kauffman, J. (1989) Intrapsychic dimensions of disenfranchised grief, in K. Doka (ed.) *Disenfranchised Grief: Recognizing Hidden Sorrow*. Lexington, MA: Lexington Books.

Martin, T.I. and Doka, K.J. (2000) *Men Don't Cry . . . Women Do: Transcending Gender Stereotypes of Grief*. Philadelphia, PA: Bruner/Mazel.

Newburn, T. (1993) *Working with Disasters: Social Welfare Interventions during and after Tragedy*. Harlow: Longman.

Rowling, L. (1995) Disenfranchised grief of teachers, *Omega: Journal of Death and Dying*, 31(4): 317–29.

CHAPTER 12

Education and training

Introduction

Research has identified the difficulties experienced by school personnel in teaching about loss and grief and handling a critical incident, and the lack of training that they may have had (Rowling and Holland 2000). A comparative study between England and Australia found that comprehensive training can have a positive impact on reducing these difficulties. In Australia, where most teachers reported some formal education about grief, more teaching and grief support were provided. In England, in contrast, there were fewer professional learning opportunities; where there was education in schools, it tended to be focused on emotional aspects surrounding teaching and learning. For example, a larger proportion of the English sample reported becoming 'less afraid of death' to be a goal of the teaching; concerns were voiced about the teaching because it was thought it would 'create anxiety' (Rowling and Holland 2000). The emotional component of loss and grief education causes great concern to teachers. It appears that education and training can reduce this. As the research reported here highlights, for education about loss and grief, there has to be both cognitive and emotional readiness and training needs to address both these aspects.

Factors that influence education and training about loss and grief

Chapter 1 identified the nature of sensitive issues in schools. This sensitivity is the result of emotion created by the interaction of the issue, a person's beliefs and experiences, the context and the meaning of the issues to the individual. Education can impact on an individual's beliefs and therefore change the meaning of issues. For example, the belief that children do not grieve may be altered by education, leading to a greater appreciation of the need to offer support, with its potential to help a young person understand and adjust to their loss. Similarly, a teacher may believe they cannot handle discussions about loss, but training can increase feelings of self-efficacy for this role. The implications for education and training of this delineation of the nature of sensitive issues are that planning for educational programmes for school personnel and those working with schools needs to be cognisant of all the elements that can create sensitivity, and information and skills need to be provided for the effective handling of these issues.

Together with the sensitivity of the area, another factor that influences education and training is the purpose of the sessions. The chapters in this book have identified a range of personnel who may benefit from learning experiences about grief and schools; that is, different educational experiences need to be designed (Stokes *et al.* 1999) depending on the desired outcomes. The learning required to raise awareness about loss and grief is quite different from that required to teach about it or to be supportive to a grieving person. Teaching and being supportive have skills components. The focus is on applying information, hence a practical element is necessary in the educational experience, rather than just the acquisition of information.

Defining the purpose of the educational experience helps to delineate the types of learning and the formats that might be useful. For example, teachers will have different learning needs in relation to grief. It is an underlying premise of the approach advocated in this book that all teachers will have a minimal understanding of grief as part of their professional role. But there are other facets to their role as teachers. In a classroom they may be educators, facilitators, protectors and carers (O'Toole 1991). As an *educator*, they convey information about loss and grief and develop skills such as being supportive, in a classroom or perhaps in small groups. They are *facilitators* of dialogue, encouraging the exchange of experiences and viewpoints in the classroom. This requires that they act as a *protector*, creating trust and safety for these discussions. Finally, a teacher may be a *carer*, offering support. Educational experiences will need to acknowledge all these different roles.

Other school personnel, such as pastoral care coordinators, heads of house or tutor groups, year coordinators, educational psychologists and school counsellors might take more responsibility for one-to-one counselling or groupwork with grieving young people. They might also be expected to be more knowledgeable and to have the ability to manage a critical incident. Consequently, they will need more in-depth information and greater skill development. Equally, skills for working with adults and knowledge about adult grief might be required of headteachers, deputies, school chaplains and faculty heads who encounter grieving parents and teachers. Similar differences in educational experiences based on the aims to be achieved can be identified for personnel outside a school system. A general practitioner might need to be made aware of the impact of adolescent losses as a background issue for medical care, whereas a bereavement counsellor would need in-depth knowledge about the management of a critical incident.

For the range of personnel who might be involved in the management of grief, the types of learning that need to be provided vary (Stokes *et al.* 1999). Although these will overlap, they can be categorized as: awareness raising, knowledge and skill development, and expansion and consolidation of expertise. A minimal amount of awareness raising about loss and grief and its impact on children and adolescents is necessary for all school personnel, including administrative and support staff, for parents and for outside service providers, including clergy and health professionals. In the long term, this may contribute to a greater acceptance and openness about grief.

In schools, teachers who conduct lessons about grief will require increased knowledge and pedagogical skills. This will require time to practise skills and the development of a personal philosophy about the learning experiences offered, as well as reflection on the curriculum, teaching and learning outcomes. A more comprehensive and broader understanding is required for teachers who counsel (McGuiness 1998) or who take on other support roles. An ability 'to recognise the ceiling of their skills and to be able to refer on appropriately' (Stokes *et al.* 1999: 302) is essential. These professionals are likely to have wide professional experience that can be built upon.

Individuals whose role demands that they possess expertise in loss and grief will require a breadth and depth of knowledge that is current. They will also need to possess highly developed counselling skills and the ability to implement a variety of therapeutic interventions for young people as well as adults. The ability to act in a supervisory role to support other professionals and act as a facilitator of the action and learning of these people is also necessary. Finally, it would be useful to have critical judgement skills to handle controversies surrounding such issues as debriefing and suicide in schools.

Just as there are different learning experiences for school personnel, different levels of skill are required of personnel outside schools. Stokes *et al.* (1999) identified these as follows:

- *Level 1*: individuals working indirectly with a bereaved child; that is, people who are part of the child's everyday environment.

- *Level 2*: trained volunteers and paid staff working directly with a bereaved child and families.
- *Level 3*: senior professional staff with specialized vocational training.

Most training in England focuses on Level 1 skills, whereas in Australia nationally funded and distributed materials developed for trainee teachers, teachers and postgraduate study are available.

Similar criteria to the above can be developed for personnel outside schools. Within the framework of partnerships advocated in this book, locally based training opportunities at the awareness raising level could offer this generic education and provide the opportunity for personnel in a local area to begin to develop links. This multidisciplinary workforce development is part of the capacity-building strategy identified in Chapter 9.

Learning formats

A discussion about the process and content of loss and grief in the school curriculum for students is provided in Chapter 4. This chapter focuses on both informal and formal learning for individuals who are involved with the teaching and support of children and adults, assisting a school to manage a critical incident and conducting bereavement support groups.

Formal learning

The learner's needs shape the purposes of the learning. Adult learning theory – andragogy, the art and science of helping adults learn (Knowles 1980) – re-shaped the form of education and training in the 1980s. The key point of this theory was that learners have personal and professional experience and come from specific social and ethnic backgrounds, which needs to be accommodated and utilized in learning. Experienced educators recognize that this is similar for young people; in the classroom, this is reflected in student-centred learning and problem-based learning. It is also an essential tenet of education and training for loss and grief. Within the levels of learning identified earlier, learning for skill development was present. Skill development requires the acquisition of competence to perform a particular task, the doing of something. In this case, the task is interaction with human beings and sensitive issues.

For example, 'self-study' through reading was reported to be the main form of professional development of teachers in England (Rowling and Holland 2000). Such learning does not provide the opportunities for sharing experiences and talking with others, particularly about sensitive issues, such as how to manage your own feelings and those of students and other bereaved individuals. The Australian sample reported greater opportunities for and experiences of professional development. They were more prepared to share personal experiences as a teaching strategy, which indicated that they were more comfortable in their role. As reported in Chapter 4, these teachers were able to articulate a philosophy about using personal experience as a teaching strategy.

Informal learning

Many opportunities exist for learning on the job, either guided by a mentor or as a result of individual reflection on experiences. Sometimes this will be incidental learning (Watkins and Marsick 1992), where the learner is not consciously aware that learning is taking place. In other instances, the learner will be aware that they are engaged in a learning process. This informal learning could take the form of 'shadowing'; this is where one person follows another around and then discusses with the person 'shadowed' events and actions. This form of learning is strengthened in an organization when the methods used and the opportunities for learning are increased. With limited time and resources in schools, voluntary and statutory organizations, informal learning would be a valuable addition to workforce development. The depth and breadth of the learning can be dependent on the events, the skill and the insight of the person being shadowed and the critical reflective skills of both people.

Engagement with learning materials

Active engagement with learning materials is necessary to assist people to be more comfortable when dealing with loss and grief issues. Ideally, a face-to-face learning format will provide this engagement, but well-structured self-learning materials with in-depth reflection on practice, documented in a journal and shared with a facilitator, might achieve similar outcomes. The aim in the interactive learning environment is not for the learner to take a passive recipient mode, but to be actively engaged with the materials. Participants will want to tell their story. This is an important learning opportunity. It allows participants to build a view of life and death according to their own story. For listeners, it provides the opportunity to learn how someone has been adversely affected, yet strength and meaning have been found in the experience. A skilled educator is sensitive to the value of this but remains cognisant of the purpose of the educational session.

Lectures are the most didactic form of learning experience. However, brief interactions between participants within the lecture can help personalise learning. Greater engagement would be aimed for in structured experiences that involve interactive activities that are reflected upon.

Content

Thoughts and feelings – the cognitive and the affective – are at the centre of education and training about loss and grief. During educational experiences, an understanding is required of the affective elements involved and skill development to support grieving people and their emotional responses. Recent work by Daniel Goleman (1995, 1998) articulates key elements of the concept of emotional intelligence. These are useful in developing an understanding of the personal qualities that need to be developed in students of loss and grief and in providing direction for the content of learning opportunities. According to Goleman, emotional intelligence includes:

- *Self-awareness* – knowing one's emotions.
- *Managing emotions* – building on self-awareness and handling feelings so that they are appropriate for a set of circumstances encountered.
- *Motivating oneself* – directing emotions to reach a goal.
- *Reading emotions* – empathizing and being sensitive to others' emotions.
- *Handling relationships* – resolving conflicts, being cooperative and problem solving.

Emotional intelligence helps to identify characteristics that need to be developed to manage grief. These characteristics help manage the emotionality for the person, the student or other client. Gail, a teacher of many years experience, in talking about what makes an effective educator alluded to emotional intelligence, although she did not label it as such:

> *I think the most satisfying thing is that they are now talking about the fact that people can be gifted in both interpersonal and intrapersonal relationships. People are beginning to acknowledge that people do have certain skills and that these skills can be very important in terms of employment opportunities. Employers are saying if you analyse it, people have to be successful individuals. They have the skills that can deal with their own intrapersonal stuff and can work cooperatively with other people.*
>
> (Gail, teacher for 14 years)

Empathy is an essential skill for supporting grieving people or educating about loss and grief. The ability to be open to others' responses is an essential requirement for adults working with children, in respecting and acknowledging the way they experience events. This requires acknowledgment of emotional responses and the range of adaptive strategies that may be used. That is, although emotional intelligence is an important concept, many people's grief responses include other behaviours and reactions.

Learning environment

A critical aspect of the learning environment that needs to be developed relates to feelings of trust, safety and security. Although not all learning environments will be emotionally charged for all participants, loss and grief can trigger distressing responses. It is incumbent on the educator to do no harm. Layers of protection need to be created.

Layers of protection

The first layer of protection may be to have two facilitators, so that there is always someone who can observe how the group is responding to the material and be able to follow up with people in the coffee breaks. Having two facilitators also offers the opportunity for a debriefing discussion at the end of the session.

A second protective layer is created by the use of judicial judgement in the choice of learning experiences and the graphic presentation of audio-visual materials. Choosing teaching approaches with the aim of triggering intense emotional responses is unethical.

A third protective layer is to forewarn participants. For example, in teaching about loss and grief to undergraduate and postgraduate students, I always warn them the week before about the content of the material, saying: 'Next week we will discuss loss and grief. There is the possibility it may trigger memories of past loss experiences or a strong emotional response'. Students have the option of not being involved. A similar process is adopted in the class. They can pass on activities and are not forced to be involved in discussions.

A fourth protective layer comes at the close of a session, when participants who may have become upset are invited to talk with the facilitator, with the view to referring them to help in the local area. It is important that the facilitator has identified this help before the session and that participants are not singled out for referral.

A fifth protective layer comes from the skill of the facilitator, who can hear the stories of the participants but remember the focus and purpose of the session. This does not mean inflexibility in presentation, rather that the facilitator is able to maintain direction and draw the storyteller's experience into the learning aims of the session.

A sixth protective layer, which is especially important when the people involved are familiar with each other, relates to the level of disclosure that people may feel comfortable with. Privacy rules about discussion outside the group and of information disclosed in the educational session need to be agreed to at the beginning and protective interrupting (a gentle caution if a participant starts adding personal details) will have to be used if necessary.

Role modelling

An educational experience provides the opportunity for all participants to learn from observing others. The facilitator needs to be aware that participants learn by what is said as well as how it is said and the manner of the interaction. Respect, caring and sensitivity can be conveyed and learnt in this manner. Observation of the facilitator being open to the experiences of participants, modelling the handling of expressions of anger and being genuine and empathic in their interactions with participants, all provide occasions for the acquisition of knowledge and concrete examples of information being covered. The words, phrases, tone of voice, use of humour and non-verbal behaviour all convey important messages to participants. The facilitator's actions can help develop feelings of confidence in participants, particularly those whose grief has been triggered; a confidence that emotional responses can be managed by individuals and by facilitators in the learning experience.

Teacher professional development

Although professional development of people outside the school environment is necessary, teachers are the main focus of this book. Introductory professional development is required for all school staff. This could begin with a session on loss and grief, followed by an additional session in secondary schools about suicide. In primary schools, teachers are the main support point for a bereaved child. Therefore, they may need additional information about how to provide ongoing care to a child and possibly a child's parent. For all staff, an initial session could focus on:

- knowledge about grief reactions;
- a review of school policies, such as critical incident management, pastoral care structures and procedures;
- an exploration of issues of privacy and confidentiality; and
- referral processes.

A follow-up session for secondary schools on suicide should:

- review mental health promotion activities in the school and place suicide prevention in that context;
- review policies about diversity, inclusiveness, the prevention of violence, bullying and harassment as well as the suicide postvention section in the critical incident management plan;
- provide information on suicide ideation and behaviour that might identify students in distress or at risk;
- identify staff roles and responsibilities, including legal requirements in responding to young people talking about committing suicide or friends expressing concern for a peer; and
- review referral pathways (Cahill 2000).

For those staff who will be teaching about loss and grief, more detailed training is required. It requires 'readiness to teach' both emotionally and content wise. In teaching loss and grief, developing the following competencies in students shapes their learning:

- knowledge about loss and grief;
- skills to use the information to help themselves;
- knowledge and skills to seek help and recognize when support will be beneficial;
- how to use the information to understand and support others; and
- how the knowledge and skills assists them to be a supportive school community member (Rowling 2000).

The extent to which students acquire the above competencies is related as much to their ability to acquire the skills as it is related to the ability and sensitivity of the teacher. Teaching about loss and grief requires the teacher to be able to switch sensitively with ease, from hearing one student's story about a loss experience to giving next week's assignment to the whole class. Various roles may need to be adopted at different times in a lesson: educator (ending a lesson by summarizing discussion), sympathetic listener (encouraging students to listen to their peer as they share their story) and carer for students who would benefit from referral. Teachers sometimes feel guilty when students get upset or cry in lessons. Setting up a procedure to manage such an occurrence needs to be done before lessons are taught, for example by saying: 'If anyone feels upset or sad about the things we discuss and does not want to stay in the classroom, you may go to [name a safe place that has already been arranged]'. This is safer than letting the student sit alone or with a friend in the playground. Follow-up with the student is necessary after the lesson.

Teachers working in the area of loss and grief should:

- have well-developed communication skills;
- be aware of grief and bereavement patterns;
- have identified their feelings about their own loss experiences;
- know the content and process of grief education;
- be aware of school policies and procedures about critical incident management;
- know how to support an upset child;
- maintain links with service providers; and
- accept loss and grief as part of life.

In creating a trusting environment, students benefit from sharing with a buddy and then as a foursome. This is less threatening than disclosure to the whole class. Discussion by the whole class may be useful as a result of a shared experience, for example an incident involving the school community or after watching a video. As described in Chapter 4, issues of privacy in the classroom need to be addressed by class rules.

Guidelines for responding to student's questions

The type of questions students ask will be shaped by their developmental age. For example, young children might be more interested in the mechanics of death and dying, which might appear quite macabre to a teacher. For example, 'How does a crematorium work?' 'How long does it take worms to eat a body?' Older students, on the other hand, might be curious about a teacher's personal beliefs about issues such as preference for cremation or burial. It is important that a teacher has either thought about and prepared a response to these questions or feels comfortable about saying they don't know but will find out or, depending on the age of students, suggest they find the answer and report back. The types of questions frequently asked include:

- Are you afraid of death?
- Do you believe in euthanasia?
- Why do people die?
- When you die do you want to be cremated, embalmed and buried, or just buried?
- Can you be frozen until a cure is found for your disease?
- My Dad and Mum are separated. My sister is going to live with Mum and Dad wants me to live with him, but I also want to be with my sister, what should I do?

In deciding how to respond, teachers need to consider the following options:

1 *Answer honestly*. This establishes your willingness to share personal viewpoints, thus modelling honesty. It removes the 'silence factor' around the topic, but also alerts students to your possible bias.
2 *Refuse to answer*. You may have agreed as a class that no-one will be required to disclose personal information (you are included in this agreement). You may wish to maintain your credibility and an honest response would weaken this and present you as an inappropriate role model, or your response may conflict with school community values.
3 *Equivocate, deflect or lie*. You may be evasive ('Is it important for you to know?' 'Would it make a difference to you how I answered?' 'How do you think your parents would respond to that question?'). Tell a story that relates to a friend ('A friend of mine believes that. . .') or simply lie (Rowling 2000).

Each one these raises certain issues depending on the setting, the class, your school community, the context of the question, who is asking and why the question is being asked. In deciding how to respond, the following should be kept in mind:

1 *Ensure educational value*. What are the motives behind your response? Are they to be seen as friendly or to meet some of your own needs about grief? The main question to ask yourself is: Will my response further the outcomes for teaching about loss and grief?
2 *Be comfortable*. Although teaching about sensitive issues such as grief can be more difficult than other topics, as you learn, read and teach about grief, any discomfort you may feel will be reduced. Your discomfort can be conveyed by avoiding particular topics students may be interested in, changing the line of discussion when emotive issues are aired and your body language.
3 *Be above board*. Act upon principles you have established in your mind from discussions with colleagues and as you prepare to teach in this area. A straightforward refusal to answer is as an appropriate response as supplying the information (Rowling 2000).

Personal disclosure

Teachers' personal disclosure is less problematic when concerned with grief than other sensitive issues such as sexuality. Research has identified that students see such disclosure as the teacher 'being human' (see Chapter 4). It does not lessen their respect for the teacher and the students believe such teachers are more likely to understand them as individuals. Teachers themselves feel that involving 'the personal' is their professional responsibility in teaching in this area and is based on sound educational principles. Their day-to-day work involves finding ways to help students understand academic topics. In teaching about loss and grief, teachers are teaching about life, so naturally their own life experiences make this learning concrete.

Students look to their teachers as role models, as examples of how adults react and behave, being open and honest and of having positive attitudes – and demonstrating that it is all right to cry and talk about feelings. Teachers need to be careful not to suggest their behaviour is the only way to act, but use their experiences as springboards for the student's own discussions. Trust and respect are important elements in these teaching–learning interactions, the teacher for the student in trusting the student's handling of personal information and the student for the teacher in respecting the teacher's right to privacy.

In the classroom, you may need to be alert to students with special needs:

- young people with an illness that could be the cause of their death (e.g. cystic fibrosis, asthma, cancer);
- young people who have experienced significant life changes or trauma that could have resulted in vulnerable emotional states;
- young people who have more chance of experiencing a major loss in the near future (e.g. a student who has a parent or sibling with a terminal illness);
- young people from particular cultural, ethnic and religious backgrounds; and
- young people with existing mental health problems or suicidal ideation.

How do students respond to lessons about grief and loss?

Students may need guidance on appropriate behaviour, both as a 'sharing student' and a 'listening student'. Much of the learning that will come from these experiential lessons takes place when the students talk and share, when they listen and hear others' thoughts and experiences, and when they reflect on how the learning can be applied to their own experiences of loss and grief. (It is important to provide students with the opportunity for personal reflection. These reflections may be shared with others or kept as private thoughts and recorded in a diary.) Prompts for personal reflection include: 'How did that feel?' 'What I have learned is . . .'. 'How does what I have heard apply to my experiences?'

Some students engage in discussions readily, sharing stories that had an impact on their lives; others are very quiet and seemingly uninvolved, but they are often thinking deeply about what they hear and about their teacher's and peers' disclosures. Being quiet does not mean uninvolved. In confronting loss experiences, students' security can be threatened. It is essential that an 'emotionally' safe environment is created for teaching and learning about loss and grief.

Students report that they are ambivalent about lessons on loss and grief. Many students use written forms of self-expression about grief (poetry, diaries, stories and songs). Females are more likely than males to use these methods. Song-writing is most frequently used to express positive emotions. A variety of methods, therefore, need to be used when teaching about loss and grief.

Resurgence of feelings phenomenon

School personnel need to be aware of how the impact of past loss experiences, especially those connected with their professional lives, can be triggered by teaching about loss and grief and supporting grieving young people. Teachers can access support for their teaching in this area by team teaching or identifying a support person who can help defuse feelings that have been triggered. Teachers have been recognized as 'disenfranchised grievers' (Chapter 11). Being affected by grief influences a teacher's view of themselves as a competent professional. This might mean teachers do not wish to teach about loss and grief. As with sex education, educating about loss and grief requires a certain amount of comfort on the teacher's part.

Frequently, current loss experiences and discussions about loss trigger thoughts and feelings about previous losses. Sometimes people are conscious of this connection, but at other times it can be at an unconscious level, particularly if the loss was traumatic or at an early developmental age. The classroom teacher may be alerted to these instances in young people by identifying what appears to be an 'over-reaction' to an event or discussion. For example, an adolescent's first broken love affair could trigger fears of abandonment experienced when parents separated when the young person was in primary school. Teachers will need to follow up on these reactions by seeking information from other staff or talking with the student or care-givers. This may by followed up by referral to the school counsellor or educational psychologist.

Conclusion

Learning about loss and grief provides participants with a new appreciation and different perspectives about life. Teachers need the ability to switch roles from educator to carer. For teachers who do take on this educator role, they do so because they see it as part of their professional responsibility, relating to students, acknowledging their experiences to enable them to feel more comfortable in the learning environment, a requirement to achieve their educational goals.

Implications for practice

- Establish protective layers for participants in educational sessions.
- All school staff need professional development opportunities for loss and grief. This should be provided at various levels depending on people's role within the school.
- It is important that those teaching about loss and grief consider how they will respond to personal questions from students.

Further reading

Goleman, D. (1998) *Working with Emotional Intelligence*. New York: Bantam Books.

Knowles, M. (1980) *The Modern Practice of Adult Education: From Pedagogy to Andragogy*. Chicago, IL: Follet.

O'Toole, D. (1991) *Growing through Grief: A K-12 Curriculum to Help Young People through all Kinds of Losses*. Burnville, NC: Compassion Books.

Stokes, J., Pennington, J., Monroe, B., Papadatou, D. and Relf, M. (1999) Developing services for bereaved children: a discussion of the theoretical and practical issues involved, *Mortality*, 4(3): 291–307.

Watkins, K.E. and Marsick, V. (1992) Towards a theory of informal and incidental learning in organisations, *International Journal of Lifelong Learning*, 11(4): 287–300.

Glossary

Bereavement: is the state or fact of realizing a loss, or the social state 'bereaved' of someone who has experienced a loss (Howarth and Leaman 2001).

Critical incident: is defined as any situation faced by members of the school community causing them to experience unusually strong emotional reactions which have the potential to interfere with their ability to function either at the time the situation arises, or later (Sheehan *et al.* 2000: 31).

Critical incident management plan or policy: contains both the technical and mechanical guidelines of an evacuation plan and arrangements for the management of personnel and their reactions. It includes preventive aspects such as risk management and education and information strategies; guidelines for management of crises; and suggestions for longer term action.

Disenfranchised grief: may arise because a relationship is not recognized; the loss is not acknowledged; society does not give the person that role; and because of the circumstances of a death and the way individuals grieve (Doka 2002).

Educational psychologist: is a person with professionally recognized training in psychology. Their skills can vary from focusing on working with children and schools, to other areas such as families and children with specific problems. They may be specialist in testing for learning and behaviour problems, and/or counselling young people one to one, or in groups and can be based in a school on a full-time or part-time basis, or in an education authority.

Faculty: describes an organizational structure in secondary schools usually based around subject areas.

Grief: is the expression of an individual's experience of loss (Howarth and Leaman 2001).

Headteacher: is the person with educational expertise in charge of a school. They are also known as the principal or headmaster/headmistress.

Indigenous people: a term used by the United Nations in its recognition of the special or unique rights of 'First Peoples' or 'First Nations' (Hurley 2001).

LEA: is an acronym for Local Education Authority.

Loss: is the state of being deprived of someone or something valued (Howarth and Leaman 2001).

Meaning making: involves personal values, perceptions and cognitions as well as family and cultural factors that influence the interpretation of a loss.

Non-English speaking background: describes young people from culturally and linguistically diverse origins who may have one or both parents or caregivers at home who do not speak English.

Outside service providers: can be statutory or non-statutory agencies and organizations, as well as individuals from a private practice. They may have formal on-going links with a school or be called upon in crisis situations.

Pastoral care: focuses on promoting the emotional and social well being within the school community. Pastoral care programmes also contribute to developing a sense of belonging. Pastoral care coordinators are sometimes known as student welfare advisers.

Professional development: is educational opportunities engaged in by trained teachers. They can be study in a formal setting such as a university or short course of hours or days duration at their school or in other settings. Also known in INSET and inservice education.

Resurgence of feelings phenomenon: occurs when feelings related to loss, which can sometimes be unresolved, are triggered by current experiences. They may appear to others to be out of place in relation to the current experience. It is often an unconscious process.

School climate: is the atmosphere in a classroom or school that influences moral, educational and social development; and individual well being. It is part of the 'hidden' curriculum or school ethos. School policies, pastoral care and disciplinary practices, cultural values and positive interpersonal relationships all influence student and staff learning and working environments.

School counsellor: is similar to an educational psychologist, but may have more emphasis on addressing young people's psychosocial needs as they impact on their academic progress. Whereas a guidance counsellor is more likely to concentrate on academic progress and career choice.

Secondary schools: also known as high schools usually cater for young people in their adolescent years. The first year age varies between 11 and 13 years. Middle schools and senior colleges (junior and senior high schools) segment the age groupings into grades, with variations in age groups involved.

Year adviser: also known as head of year or form patron, are teachers in a secondary school responsible for a specific year cohort. Duties could be administrative, monitoring academic progress; liaising with caregivers; linking with support personnel inside and outside the school; and offering personal support to students. Year coordinators are more likely to be involved in administration and educational matters for their cohort.

Young people: is as a generic term used in this text for both children and adolescents. Some texts use the term to refer only to adolescents.

References

Anderson, M., Kaufman, J., Simon, T.R. *et al.* (2001) School-associated violent deaths in the United States, 1994–1999, *Journal of the American Medical Association*, 286(21): 2695–702.

Antonovsky, A. (1987) *Unravelling the Mystery of Health: How People Manage Stress and Stay Well.* San Francisco, CA: Jossey-Bass.

Averill, J.R. and Nunley, E.P. (1988) Grief as an emotion and as a disease: a social-constructionist perspective, *Journal of Social Issues*, 44(3): 79–95.

Balk, D.E. (1983) Effects of sibling death on teenagers, *Journal of School Health*, 15: 14–18.

Balk, D.E. (1991) Death and adolescent bereavement: current research and future directions, *Journal of Adolescent Research*, 6(1): 7–27.

Bandura, A. (1986) *Social Foundations of Thought and Action.* Englewood Cliffs, NJ: Prentice-Hall.

Barnard, P., Morland, I. and Nagy, J. (1999) *Children, Bereavement and Trauma: Nurturing Resilience.* London: Jessica Kingsley.

Benard, B. (1995) *Fostering Resilience in Children: ERIC Digest.* Urbano, IL: ERIC: Clearinghouse on Elementary and Early Childhood Education.

Berger, P. and Luckman, T. (1967) *The Social Construction of Reality: A Treatise on the Sociology of Knowledge.* London: Penguin.

Berman, A.L. and Jobes, D.A. (1997) *Adolescent Suicide Assessment and Intervention.* Washington, DC: American Psychological Society.

Birrell Wiesen, R. and Orley, J. (1996) *Life Skills Education: Planning for Research*, WHO/MNH/PSF/96.2Rev.2. Geneva: World Health Organization.

Bluebond-Langner, M. (1996) *In the Shadow of Illness: Parents and Siblings of the Chronically Ill.* Princeton, NJ: Princeton University Press.

Bullivant, R. (1998) Bereavement and loss: the primary school context. Unpublished doctoral dissertation, University of Hull.

Cahill, H. (ed.) (2000) *Educating for Life: A Guide for School-based Responses to Preventing Self-harm and Suicide.* Canberra: Commonwealth Department of Health and Aged Care (available at http://www.curriculum.edu.au/mindmatters).

Centers for Disease Control (1988) Recommendations for the community plan for the prevention and containment of suicide clusters, *Morbidity and Mortality Weekly*, 37: S1–S6.

Centers for Disease Control (1992) *Youth Suicide Prevention Programs: A Resource Guide*. Atlanta, GA: Centers for Disease Control.

Christ, G.H. (2000) *Healing Children's Grief*. Oxford: Oxford University Press.

Cohen, S. and Syme, S.L. (1985) *Social Support and Health*. Orlando, FL: Academic Press.

Commonwealth Department of Health and Family Services (1997) *Youth Suicide in Australia: The National Youth Suicide Prevention Strategy*. Canberra: AGPS.

Corr, C. (1998–99) Enhancing the concept of disenfranchised grief, *Omega: Journal of Death and Dying*, 38(1): 1–20.

Corr, C. and Balk, D. (eds) (1996) *Handbook of Adolescent Death and Bereavement*. New York: Springer.

Criniti, D. (2001) *Duty of Care in New South Wales Schools*. Unpublished paper, Faculty of Education, University of Sydney.

Cutrona, C.E., Suhr, J.A. and MacFarlane, R. (1990) Interpersonal transactions and the psychological sense of support, in S. Duck (ed.) *Personal Relationships and Social Support*. London: Sage.

Davies, B. (1999) *Shadows in the Sun: The Experiences of Sibling Bereavement in Childhood*. Philadelphia, PA: Bruner/Mazel.

Deaton, R.L. and Berkan, W.A. (1995) *Planning and Managing Death Issues in the Schools*. Westport, CT: Greenwood Press.

Deveau, E.J. (1995) Perceptions of death through the eyes of children, in D.W. Adams and E.J. Deveau (eds) *Beyond the Innocence of Childhood: Factors Influencing Children's and Adolescent's Perceptions and Attitudes towards Death*, Vol. 1. New York: Baywood.

Doka, K. (ed.) (1989) *Disenfranchised Grief: Recognizing Hidden Sorrow*. Lexington, MA: Lexington Books.

Doka, K. (ed.) (2002) *Disenfranchised Grief: New Directions, Challenges and Strategies for Practice*. Champaign, IL: Research Press.

Doka, K. and Martin, T. (2002) How we grieve: culture, class and gender, in *Disenfranchised Grief: New Directions, Challenges and Strategies for Practice*. Champaign, IL: Research Press.

Dyregrov, A. (1991) *Grief in Children: A Handbook for Adults*. London: Jessica Kingsley.

Eddy, J.M. and Alles, W.F. (1983) *Death Education*. St Louis, MO: C.V. Mosby.

Egan, G. (1994) *The Skilled Helper*, 5th edn. Pacific Grove, CA: Brooks/Cole.

Galloway, D. (1990) *Pupil Welfare and Counselling: An Approach to Personal and Social Education across the Curriculum*. London: Longman.

Gary, J. and Remolino, L. (2000) Coping with loss and grief through on-line support groups, in J. Bloom and G. Walz (eds) *Cybercounseling and Cyberlearning: Strategies and Resources for the Millennium*. Alexandria, VA: American Counselling Association.

Glassock, G. and Rowling, L. (1992) *Learning to Grieve: Life Skills for Coping with Losses*. Newtown: Millennium Press.

Goleman, D. (1995) *Emotional Intelligence*. New York: Bantam Books.

Goleman, D. (1998) *Working with Emotional Intelligence*. New York: Bantam Books.

Gray, R. (1989) Adolescents' perceptions of social support after the death of a parent, *Journal of Psychosocial Oncology,* 7(3): 127–44.

Hargreaves, A., Lieberman, A., Fullan, M. and Hopkins, D. (1998) *International Handbook of Educational Change.* Boston, MA: Kluwer Academic.

Hawe, P., King, L., Noort, M., Jordens, C. and Lloyd, B. (2000) *Indicators to Help Build Capacity in Health Promotion.* Sydney: New South Wales Health Department (available at http://www.health.nsw.gov.au).

Hazell, P. and King, R. (1996) Arguments for and against teaching suicide prevention in schools, *Australian and New Zealand Journal of Psychiatry,* 30: 633–42.

Hendren, R., Birrell Weisen, R. and Orley, J. (1994) *Mental Health Programs in Schools.* Geneva: Division of Mental Health, World Health Organization.

Howarth, G. and Leaman, O. (eds) (2001) *Encyclopedia of Death and Dying.* London: Routledge.

Hurley, J. (2001) *Community Matters: Working with Diversity for Wellbeing.* Canberra: Commonwealth of Australia.

Janoff-Bulman, R. (1989) Assumptive worlds and the stress of traumatic events: applications of the schema construct, *Social Cognition,* 7(2): 113–36.

Johnson, K. (1989) *Trauma in the Lives of Children.* Claremont, CA: Hunter House.

Johnson, K. (1993) *School Crisis Management: A Hands on Guide for Training Crisis Response Teams.* Alameda, CA: Hunter House.

Kalafat, J. and Elias, M.J. (1995) Suicide prevention in an educational context: broad and narrow foci, *Suicide and Life Threatening Behaviour,* 25(1): 123–33.

Kamins, J. and Lipton, H. (1996) Crisis intervention teams: a model for schools, in R.G. Stevenson and E.P. Stevenson (eds) *Teaching Students About Death: A Comprehensive Resource for Educators and Parents.* Philalelphia, PA: Charles Press.

Kauffman, J. (1989) Intrapsychic dimensions of disenfranchised grief, in K. Doka (ed.) *Disenfranchised Grief: Recognizing Hidden Sorrow.* Lexington, MA: Lexington Books.

Klass, D., Silverman, P.R. and Nickman, S.L. (1996) *Continuing Bonds, New Understandings of Grief.* Washington, DC: Taylor & Francis.

Klicker, R.L. (2000) *A Student Dies, a School Mourns.* Philadelphia, PA: Taylor & Francis.

Knowles, M. (1980) *The Modern Practice of Adult Education: From Pedagogy to Andragogy.* Chicago, IL: Follet.

LaGrande, L.E. (1988) *Changing Patterns of Human Existence: Assumptions, Beliefs and Coping with the Stress of Change.* Springfield, IL: Charles C. Thomas.

Lattanzi-Licht, M. (2002) Grief and the workplace: positive approaches, in K.J. Doka (ed.) *Disenfranchised Grief: New Directions, Challenges and Strategies for Practice.* Champaign, IL: Research Press.

Leaman, O. (1995) *Death and Loss: Compassionate Approaches in the Classroom.* London: Cassell.

Leatham, G. and Duck, S. (1990) Conversations with friends and the dynamics of social support, in S. Duck (ed.) *Personal Relationships and Social Support.* London: Sage.

Leenaars, A.A. and Wenckstern, S. (1998) Principles of postvention: application to suicide and trauma in schools, *Death Studies,* 22(4): 357–91.

Lindsay, B. and Elsegood, J. (eds) (1996) *Working with Children in Grief and Loss.* London: Baillere Tindall.

McGuiness, J. (1998) *Counselling in Schools: New Perspectives*. London: Cassell.

MacIntyre, S. and Ellaway, A. (1999) Local opportunity structures, social capital and social inequalities in health: what can central and local government do?, *Health Promotion Journal of Australia*, 9(3): 165–70.

Mallon, B. (1998) *Helping Children Manage Loss: Positive Strategies for Renewal and Growth*. London: Jessica Kingsley.

Marris, P. (1975) *Loss and Change*. New York: Anchor Press Doubleday.

Martin, T.I. and Doka, K.J. (2000) *Men Don't Cry . . . Women Do: Transcending Gender Stereotypes of Grief*. Philadelphia, PA: Bruner/Mazel.

Mitchell, J.T. and Everly, G.S. (2000) Critical incident stress management and critical incident stress debriefings: evolutions, effects and outcomes, in B. Raphael and J.P. Wilson (eds) *Psychological Debriefing: Theory, Practice and Evidence*. New York: Cambridge University Press.

Nader, K.O. (1996) Children's exposure to traumatic experiences, in C.A. Corr and D.E. Balk (eds) *Handbook of Adolescent Death and Bereavement*. New York: Springer.

Nader, K. and Pynoos, R. (1993) School disaster: planning and initial interventions, *Journal of Social Behavior and Personality*, 8(5): 299–320.

National Health and Medical Research Council Health Advancement Standing Committee on Supportive Environments (1996) *Effective School Health Promotion: Towards Health Promoting Schools*. Canberra: AGPS.

Newburn, T. (1993) *Working with Disasters: Social Welfare Interventions during and after Tragedy*. Harlow: Longman.

New South Wales Board of Studies (1991) *Personal Development, Health and Physical Education Years 7–10: Support Document*. North Sydney: New South Wales Board of Studies.

New South Wales Cancer Council (2000) *Kids and Cancer: A Handbook for Teachers*. Sydney: New South Wales Cancer Council (available at http://www.nswcc.org.au).

New South Wales Health Department (2001) *A Framework for Building the Capacity to Improve Health*. Sydney: New South Wales Health Department (available at http://www.health.nsw.gov.au).

O'Connor-Fleming, M.L. and Parker, E. (2001) *Health Promotion: Principles and Practices in the Australian Context*, 2nd edn. Sydney: Allen & Unwin.

Oltjenbruns, K.A. (1996) Death of a friend during adolescence: issues and impact, in C.A. Corr and D.E. Balk (eds) *Handbook of Adolescent Death and Bereavement*. New York: Springer.

O'Toole, D. (1991) *Growing through Grief: A K-12 Curriculum to Help Young People through all Kinds of Losses*. Burnville, NC: Compassion Books.

Pardeck, J. (1994) Using literature to help adolescents cope with problems, *Adolescence*, 29(114): 421–7.

Parkes, C.M. (1988) Bereavement as a psychosocial transition: processes of adaptation to change, *Journal of Social Issues*, 44(3): 53–65.

Petersen, S. and Straub, R.L. (1992) *School Crisis Survival Guide: Management Techniques and Materials for Counsellors and Administrators*. West Nyack, NY: Centre for Applied Research in Education.

Pfefferbaum, B., Nixon, S.J., Tucker, P.M. *et al.* (1999) Posttraumatic stress responses in bereaved children after the Oklahoma City bombing, *Journal of the American Academy of Child and Adolescent Psychiatry*, 38(11): 1372–9.

Plant, S. and Stoate, P. (1989) *Loss and Change: Resources for Use in Personal and Social Education Programmes.* Crediton: Southgate.

Raphael, B. (1985) *Anatomy of Bereavement.* London: Hutchinson.

Raphael, B. and Wilson J.P. (eds) (2000) *Psychological Debriefing: Theory, Practice and Evidence.* New York: Cambridge University Press.

Reed, M.L. (2000) *Grandparents Cry Twice.* New York: Baywood.

Ringler, L.L. and Hayden, D.C. (2000) Adolescent bereavement and social support: peer loss compared to other loss, *Journal of Adolescent Research,* 15(2): 209–30.

Robinson, R. (2000) Debriefing with emergency services: critical incident stress management, in B. Raphael and J.P. Wilson (eds) *Psychological Debriefing: Theory, Practice and Evidence.* New York: Cambridge University Press.

Robinson, R. and Mitchell, J.T. (1993) Evaluation of psychological debriefing, *Journal of Traumatic Stress,* 6: 367–82.

Rosenblatt, P.C. (1988) Grief: the social context of private feelings, *Journal of Social Issues,* 44(3): 67–78.

Rosenblatt, P. (2000) *Parent Grief: Narratives of Loss and Relationship.* Philadelphia, PA: Bruner/Mazel.

Rowling, L. (1994) Loss and grief in the context of the health promoting school. Unpublished doctoral dissertation, University of Southampton.

Rowling, L. (1995) Disenfranchised grief of teachers, *Omega: Journal of Death and Dying,* 31(4): 317–29.

Rowling, L. (1996a) A comprehensive approach to handling sensitive issues in schools with special reference to loss and grief, *Pastoral Care in Education,* 4(1): 17–21.

Rowling, L. (1996b) Learning about life: teaching about loss, in R. Best (ed.) *Education Spirituality and the Whole Child.* London: Cassell.

Rowling, L. (1999) The role of policy in creating a supportive social context for the management of loss experiences and critical incidents in school communities, *Crisis, Illness and Loss,* 7(3): 252–65.

Rowling, L. (2000) *MindMatters: A Whole School Approach to Loss and Grief.* Canberra: Department of Health and Aged Care (available at http://www.curriculum.edu.au/mindmatters).

Rowling, L. (2002) Youth and disenfranchised grief, in K.J. Doka (ed.) *Disenfranchised Grief: New Directions, Challenges and Strategies for Practice.* Champaign, IL: Research Press.

Rowling, L. and Burr, A. (1997) Creating supportive environments, in D. Colquhoun, K. Goltz and M. Sheehan (eds) *The Health Promoting School: Policy, Programmes and Practice in Australia.* Marrickville: Harcourt Brace.

Rowling, L. and Holland, J. (2000) Grief and school communities: the impact of social context, a comparison between Australia and England, *Death Studies,* 24(1): 15–24.

Rowling, L., Martin, G. and Walker, L. (2002) *Mental Health Promotion and Young People: Concepts and Practice.* Sydney: McGraw-Hill.

Rutter, M. (1995) *Psychological Disturbances in Young People: Challenges for Prevention.* Cambridge: Cambridge University Press.

Schmitt, R.L. and Ellman, T.D. (1991) Devaluating death education through short term teen suicide intervention programs, *Omega: Journal of Death and Dying,* 24: 241–5.

Schwartzberg, S.S. and Janoff-Bulman, R. (1991) Grief and the search for meaning: exploring the assumptive worlds of bereaved college students, *Journal of Social and Clinical Psychology*, 10: 270–88.

Shaffer, D., Vieland, V., Garland, A. *et al.* (1990) Adolescent suicide attempters: response to suicide prevention programs, *Journal of the American Medical Association*, 264: 3151–5.

Shears, J. (1995) Managing tragedy in a secondary school, in S.C. Smith and S.M. Pennells (eds) *Interventions with Bereaved Children*. London: Jessica Kingsley.

Sheehan, M., Marshall, B., Cahill, H., Rowling, L. and Holdsworth, R. (2000) *SchoolMatters: Mapping and Managing Mental Health in Schools*. Canberra: Commonwealth Department of Health and Aged Care (available at http://www.curriculum.edu.au/mindmatters).

Silverman, P.R. (2000) *Never too Young to Know: Death in Children's Lives*. New York: Oxford University Press.

Skewes, K. (1999) Teenagers, music and grief: making the connection. Paper presented to the NALAG 11th National Conference, Melbourne, 21 October.

Smilansky, S. (1987) *On Death: Helping Children Understand and Cope*. New York: Peter Lang.

Smith, C.C. and Pennells, M. (eds) (1995) *Interventions with Bereaved Children*. London: Jessica Kingsley.

Smith, S. and Pennels, M. (1994) *The Forgotten Mourners*. London: Jessica Kingsley.

Stallard, P. (2000) Debriefing adolescents after critical life events, in B. Raphael and J.P. Wilson (eds) *Psychological Debriefing: Theory, Practice and Evidence*. New York: Cambridge University Press.

Stein, A.J. and Winokuer, H.R. (1989) Monday morning: managing employee grief, in K. Doka (ed.) *Disenfranchised Grief: Recognizing Hidden Sorrow*. Lexington, MA: Lexington Books.

Stevenson, R.G. (1996) If this is supposed to be the best time of my life why do I feel so rotten? Questions and answers about adolescent suicide and loss, in R.G. Stevenson and E.P. Stevenson (eds) *Teaching Students about Death: A Comprehensive Resource for Educators and Parents*. Philadelphia, PA: Charles Press.

Stokes, J., Pennington, J., Monroe, B., Papadatou, D. and Relf, M. (1999) Developing services for bereaved children: a discussion of the theoretical and practical issues involved, *Mortality*, 4(3): 291–307.

Stroebe, M.S., Stroebe, W. and Hansson, R.O. (eds) (1993) *Handbook of Bereavement: Theory, Research and Intervention*, 2nd edn. Cambridge: Cambridge University Press.

Stroebe, W. (2000) *Social Psychology and Health*, 2nd edn. Buckingham: Open University Press.

Tyson-Rawson, K.J. (1996) Adolescent responses to the death of a parent, in C.A. Corr and D.E. Balk (eds) *Handbook of Adolescent Death and Bereavement*. New York: Springer.

Vachon, M.L.S. and Stylianos, S.K. (1988) The role of social support in bereavement, *Journal of Social Issues*, 44(3): 175–90.

Ward, B. and Houghton, P. (1988) *Good Grief: Talking and Learning about Loss and Death*. London: Jessica Kingsley.

Wass, H., Miller, M.D. and Thornton, G. (1990) Death education, grief/suicide intervention in public schools, *Death Studies*, 14: 253–68.

Watkins, K.E. and Marsick, V. (1992) Towards a theory of informal and incidental learning in organisations, *International Journal of Lifelong Learning*, 11(4): 287–300.

Weare, K. (2000) *Promoting Mental, Emotional and Social Health: A Whole School Approach*. London: Routledge.

Weekes, D. and Johnson, C. (1992) A second decade of high school death education, *Death Studies*, 16(3): 269–79.

Willcock, D. (1996) Impressions from an Englishman on death education in the United States, in R.G. Stevenson and E.P. Stevenson (eds) *Teaching Students about Death: A Comprehensive Resource for Educators and Parents*. Philadelphia, PA: Charles Press.

Worden, J.W. (1996) *Grief and Children: When a Parent Dies*. New York: Guilford Press.

Worden, W. (1991) *Grief Counselling and Grief Therapy*, 2nd edn. New York: Springer Publication.

World Health Organization (1992) *Psychosocial Consequences of Disasters: Prevention and Management*. Geneva: World Health Organization.

World Health Organization (1993) *Life Skills Education in Schools*. WHO/MNH/ PSF/93.A Rev.1 Geneva: World Health Organization.

Wraith, R. (2000) Children and debriefing: theory, interventions and outcomes, in B. Raphael and J.P. Wilson (eds) *Psychological Debriefing: Theory, Practice and Evidence*. New York: Cambridge University Press.

Yule, W. (1989) The effects of disasters on children, *Association for Child Psychology and Psychiatry*, 11: 3–6.

Yule, W. and Gold, A. (1993) *Wise Before the Event: Coping with Crises in Schools*. London: Calouste Gulbenkian Foundation.

Zisook, S. (ed.) (1987) *Biopsychosocial Aspects of Bereavement*. Washington, DC: American Psychiatric Press.

Index